Praise for
Prodependence

"Removing codependence and addiction from the list of diseases that afflict humankind and seeing their cause as responses to overwhelming life conditions rehumanizes those who suffer—both addicts and those who love them. This approach rightly acknowledges them as co-participants in the human journey rather than objects of analysis and treatment. In *Prodependence*, Robert Weiss has not only created a new term but has also boldly challenged the cultural practice of negatively labeling those in service to others. He shows that by doing so, we devalue their selfless efforts and amplify their suffering. This groundbreaking book is a call to awaken from the old way of thinking to find new and positive methods. We recommend it to all mental health providers and to those whose mental health will improve by reading it."

—**Harville Hendrix, PhD**, and **Helen LaKelly Hunt, PhD**,
coauthors of *Getting the Love You Want*
and *The Space Between*

"At last, a therapist who understands the power of love. Bravo, Robert Weiss! Rather than judging the caregivers of addicts as codependents with pathologies of their own, Weiss recognizes them as normal, mentally healthy men and women with a deep and unconditional love for their addicted partner or family member. He celebrates emotional dependence, offering nonjudgmental support and guidance for navigating the difficult landscape of relationship with an addict. By coming from a positive perspective, his concepts offer hope instead of despair for those living in crisis. And as a bonus, it's a fascinating read about the evolution of the recovery movement, and the importance of human kindness and connection in healing."

—**Helen Fisher, PhD**, bestselling author of
Why We Love, Anatomy of Love, and
Why Him? Why Her?

"Rob Weiss is a clinical pioneer and innovator. In *Prodependence*, he takes issue with the codependence model and replaces it with an attachment-based perspective that is less pathologizing and stigmatizing of an individual or a family's love for an addicted relative. Weiss' work and speculation based on his clinical experience moves the field forward and provides clinicians who work with addictions a lot of "food for thought."

—**Christine A. Courtois, PhD, ABPP**, author,
Healing the Incest Wound and *Treating Complex Traumatic Stress Disorders* (co-authored with Dr. Julian Ford)

"*Prodependence* provides a refreshing, empathetic, and practical approach to understanding partners and families of addicts, and how best to help them learn how to handle their difficult situation. Avoiding the classic split between the trauma and codependency models, Weiss uses the framework of *attachment theory* to avoid blaming partners and pathologizing their behavior. Instead, he validates and reframes their efforts and provides techniques to help them heal, improve their self-care, set appropriate boundaries for their own behavior, and deal with their challenges. This beautifully written book is must-reading for all those who love an addict, as well as all mental health professionals."

—**Jennifer Schneider, MD**,
author of *Back from Betrayal: Recovering from the Trauma of Infidelity*

"First there was codependence, then there was the trauma model. Now we have prodependence—the evolution of empowerment for partners, families, and others affected by the addiction or illness of someone they love. Bravo, Rob Weiss, for crossing the next frontier in addiction-attachment-systems theory and extending us an invitation and detailed map of how to join him there. With fresh ideas and crisp writing, Weiss distills decades of experience into a compassionate call to action. There is a new and better way to support those whose lives are affected by an addict, and it's called prodependence."

—**Staci Sprout, LICSW, CSAT**, author of
Naked in Public: A Memoir of Recovery from Sex Addiction and Other Temporary Insanities

PRODEPENDENCE

Moving Beyond
Codependency

Robert Weiss, PhD, MSW

Health Communications, Inc.
Deerfield Beach, Florida

www.hcibooks.com

**Library of Congress Cataloging-in-Publication Data
is available through the Library of Congress**

© 2018 Robert Weiss

ISBN-13: 978-07573-2035-4 (Paperback)
ISBN-10: 07573-2035-X (Paperback)
ISBN-13: 978-07573-2036-1 (ePub)
ISBN-10: 07573-2036-8 (ePub)

Publisher: Health Communications, Inc.
          3201 S.W. 15th Street
          Deerfield Beach, FL 33442–8190

Cover design by Jim Pollard
Interior design and formatting by Lawna Patterson Oldfield

This book is dedicated to the memory of my mother, Elizabeth R. Weiss, a woman who struggled all her life (and mine) with profound bipolar disorder, unrelenting narcissism, paranoia, and psychosis. She was a brilliant mind, but also one too deeply scarred by mental illness for her to ever reach her potential as a woman, as a thinker, and as a mother. Perhaps due to her deficits, she was my greatest and longest-running pro-dependence teacher. This is true despite forty-five years of illness, hospitals, emergency rooms, abuse, detachment, enabling, caregiving, rescuing, and broken promises on both sides. This is true despite our many related emotional struggles, some of which still haunt me to this day. And this is true despite all the needed therapy, personal growth, addictions, and losses stemming from that deeply flawed mother/son relationship.

You see, no matter what any therapist, support group or anyone else ever reflected to me, that troubled woman will always be my mom. And I, her son. And within that structure, we both did our broken best to love one another through to the end. Thus I'm grateful to have been the one whispering words of peace to her in her last moments. Sadly, due to mental illness, my mother lacked both the tools and the resilience to thrive and enjoy her life (and those of her children). And yet, despite all her deficits and challenges, this woman managed to offer me just enough to be able to survive until I could find my own path to move from surviving to thriving. Thank you, Mom. This one's for you.

Contents

Contents

Acknowledgments

Prodependence is a new concept, but there are many people whose ideas, beliefs, and personal and professional support led to the writing and release of this book. In recognition of this, I wish to acknowledge the following individuals:

- First and foremost, love and thanks to my husband of eighteen years, Jonathan Michael Westerman, who is my rock and personal teacher of all things prodependent.

- Claudia Black, Melody Beattie, Pia Mellody, Robin Norwood, and all the other progenitors of the codependency field. My deep thanks to you for helping so many people in so many important ways, and for laying out a strong-enough path that I may humbly follow in your footsteps, working to forge a new path toward healing.

- Dr. Omar Minwalla, Sylvia Jason, Jerry Goodman, Dr. Stefanie Carnes, Dr. Christine Courtois, Dorit Reichental, Dr. Barbara Steffens, and everyone else who has helped to evolve the treatment of *betrayal trauma*. All of you make a profound difference and, at one point or another, you have all focused my brain toward prodependence.

- Dr. Susan Swanson, Dr. Carol Clark, Charlie Risien, Belinda Berman, Dr. Sophia Caudle, Keith Arnold, Cheryl Brown, Karen Brownd, Dee McGraw, Judy Beshella, Dr. David Fawcett (and anyone that I sadly forgot to mention). Thank you for your help with this book (and your involvement in my PhD). You've helped "Dr. Rob" become a reality. And I never saw that coming!

- My work team: Scott Brassart, Stuart Leviton, and Tami Ver-Helst. Where would I be without you? I am forever grateful for your loving support and guidance. You have helped me learn what real support feels like. Thank you one and all.

- Diana Lombardi, Annette Banca, Tori Sichta, Fiona Paladino, and the rest of the team at 5WPR. You guys rock it every day.

- HCI books. For your encouragement and brilliant insights, especially my amazing editor Christine Belleris, along with Christian Blonshine, Peter Vegso, and Kim Weiss.

- The US Journal conference team for your unending support, in particular Gary Seidler, Dan Barmettler, Suzanne Smith, and Lorrie Keip.

- Lastly and most importantly, I must thank the thousands of addicts and loved ones of addicts who've shared their pain, their triumphs, and their stories with me during my nearly three decades as a psychotherapist. My commitment to you always is to strive to decrease stigma and increase all of our chances to live meaningful lives, unfettered by addiction.

Preface

This Abstract, which I now publish,
must necessarily be imperfect ... and I must trust
to the reader reposing some confidence in my accuracy.
No doubt errors will have crept in, though I hope
I have always been cautious in trusting to good authorities alone.
I can here give only the general conclusions at which I have
arrived, with a few facts in illustration, but which, I hope,
in most cases will suffice. No one can feel more sensible than
I do of the necessity of hereafter publishing in detail all the facts,
with references, on which my conclusions have been grounded;
and I hope in a future work to do this.[1]

—Charles Darwin, *The Origin of Species*

In 1909, Charles Darwin published his now-acknowledged masterwork, *The Origin of Species*, with an introduction (excerpted above) stating that his book was, more than anything else, his opinion, with that opinion based primarily on his experience and observations as a naturalist, geologist, and biologist. He hoped that his theories would be received and investigated by other scientists with an open mind. At the same time, he knew that his ideas were likely to be met with resistance on many fronts.

And that is what came to pass. Even today, more than a century later, with oodles of research supporting the theory of evolution, *The Origin of Species* is viewed as blasphemy by a significant segment of the world's population. That said, I suspect that if Darwin were alive today to witness the still-ongoing creationism versus evolution debate, he would not in any way regret the publication of his work. I think he might say, "If we do not push forth and test new theories, we do not learn and grow."

With the publication of *Prodependence: Moving Beyond Codependency*, I find myself in a similar circumstance—pushing forth a strong opinion based on preliminary investigation and my personal experience and observations as a seasoned addiction therapist. As with *The Origin of Species*, *Prodependence* draws on a considerable amount of existing research; however, it is not a research-based or research-driven book. Rather, this book reflects my evolving views and opinions regarding addiction treatment, sourced in clinical literature, along with personal and clinical experience. No more, no less. Moreover, like Darwin, I fully expect that plenty of people will disagree with what I have to say. That's the nature of the beast.

When my colleague and early mentor Patrick Carnes published *Out of the Shadows*, the first book on sexual addiction, a few people embraced his theories, but plenty of others attacked him. The same was true with the beginnings of the trauma movement, humanistic psychotherapy, and lots of other interesting and occasionally brilliant ideas. Some people embraced these new ideas, tested them, and, if the research turned out as hypothesized, validated them.

Other people did not, opting instead to cling to old ideas even if those ideas were outdated and not useful.

But here's the deal: If no one risks new ideas, we stagnate rather than progress. I truly believe that. I also understand that leading with new ideas, especially ideas that may disrupt existing norms, is to risk ridicule, derision, and disdain. So, with this book I take an informed risk. That said, I hope you will read what I have to say with an open mind, understanding that it was written with a focus toward improving how we treat and support one another and not, in any way, to diminish ideas put forth by other people who were writing in a different time.

I sincerely hope that some readers will be interested enough in the concept of prodependence to conduct the necessary research that will prove my theories either correct or incorrect. Perhaps, over time, the risk I take here will be rewarded by our learning to better serve those we are tasked to treat—or maybe not. The ideas are here; their proofs lie ahead.

Note: I have focused this book primarily toward addicts and loved ones of addicts because those are the populations I have worked with for nearly thirty years, and the people I believe to be most in need of new treatment methods today. I nonetheless believe the tenets of prodependence as discussed in this text, rooted as they are in attachment theory, are sound when extended to any type of mutually dependent relationship. Thus, it is my hope that prodependence will resonate and encourage all readers to remain healthfully committed to looking out for (and hanging in there with) those they love—especially when times get tough.

I am not certain that everything I've written in these pages is as accurate, succinct, clear, and useful as I would like. In truth, I began working on this project nearly three years ago, and even as I write this preface, my theories and ideas are evolving. Thus, I will no doubt find myself looking back at this text in a year or two and saying things like, "Wow, I wish I'd stated that sentence/idea/example/concept differently."

So be it.

I recognize and accept that this book will not be perfect or even a fully finished product. And that is okay because my goal here is not to dazzle but to spark interest, discussion, analysis, experimentation, and, hopefully, in time, a modicum of much needed psychotherapeutic progress. My sole aim is to push the addiction treatment field (and perhaps psychotherapy as a whole) forward a step by focusing less on individual brokenness and more on inherent human strengths and attachments. If I accomplish nothing more than that, I will be happy with this work.

Chapter One

ADDICTION, EMPATHY, AND PSYCHOTHERAPY

*For full emotional communication, one person needs to allow
his mind to be influenced by that of the other.*[1]

—Daniel Siegel, *The Developing Mind*

RIDDLE ME THIS

I f my beloved wife of twelve years received a cancer diagnosis and we had two kids under the age of seven, would anyone label or judge me for doing everything possible—even to the point of giving up important parts of my life—to keep my family stable and relatively happy? If I took on two jobs, quit my exercise program, resigned from the company softball team, and stopped seeing friends to address this unexpected family crisis, would anyone in my life call me out as *enmeshed* or *enabling*? And if I went to a therapist for support, would my therapist ask me to explore the ways in which my dysfunctional childhood might be pushing me into an "unhealthy obsession" with my wife's cancer diagnosis?

Of course not.

To push this example a bit further, what if my wife refused to accept the traditional medical route to healing, deciding instead to rely on unproven herbal treatments? In that situation, should I support my wife's attempts to heal "her own way" even if I disagree? Should I spend every waking moment trying to convince her to trust Western medicine? Should I try to slip prescribed but unwanted medications into her tea when she's not looking? And if I did any or all those things, would the people in my life think of me as overreactive? Would they think that my family commitment was a negative manifestation of my traumatic past? Or would they have empathy and compassion for my grief, my fear, and my unshakable commitment to someone I love?

To be honest, I have no idea how I would act under those circumstances. I might make the right decisions. I might make the wrong decisions. Either way, I know that I would be doing the very best I could to help my spouse heal and to care for my children. And I wouldn't let anyone—friends, family, my employer, a member of the clergy, my therapist, or anyone else—tell me that my attempts to help were borne out of anything but healthy love and attachment.

Of course, nobody in my world would try to tell me otherwise. Instead, friends and family would show up on my doorstep with flowers, home-cooked meals, and sincere offers to help with childcare, shopping, yard work, and housecleaning. Meanwhile, my therapist, clergy, and employer would understand and accept that my family is in crisis, that I love them, and that I must give of myself in an extraordinary way, even if that looks a little obsessed or makes me seem a bit nutty at times. And if any of these supportive individuals felt that I was overdoing my attempts at caregiving, possibly to my own or my family's detriment, they would not chastise me. Instead, they would nudge me toward caring for myself as well as my family while offering gentle advice about how I might care for my loved ones more effectively. They wouldn't stand back and judge me; they would lean in to help.

In my world, people who take time out of their own lives to help an ailing or physically disabled loved one are called saints. They are amazing, wonderful, and special.

Unfortunately, things are different when it comes to addiction.

In contrast to the story above, let's say my spouse of twelve years became addicted to alcohol and prescription painkillers. Let's say she lost her job because she was drunk and high at work. Let's say that because of her addiction, I can no longer trust her to adequately care for our kids. What happens now when I take that second job, stop going to the gym, stop hanging out with friends, eliminate my recreational activities, and start to obsess about her drinking and using, all while paying the family bills and caring for our children? Will my friends and family, my employer, my clergy, and my therapist support this degree of caregiving and caretaking while empathizing with my frustration and exhaustion?

Most likely they will not.

In the addiction world, support and therapy for the loving spouse or parent of an addict typically involves judgmental head-shaking, *tut-tuts*, and expressions of concern about the caretaker's problem, with that problem being identified as dysfunctional attempts to love, save, rescue, and heal the addict and the family.

Move over empathy; make way for judgment.

Addiction is a universe where caregiving is often viewed as enmeshed, enabling, and controlling, and choosing to stick with an addicted loved one is seen more as a reflection of the caregiver's troubled past—meaning unresolved early-life trauma and abandonment issues—than an indication of love and healthy bonding.

This does not make sense to me, and it troubles me deeply. If I love someone with a physical illness or a disability by helping that person and the rest of my family, even to my detriment, I'm a saint. But if I love and care for an addict in the same way, I am called out as enmeshed, enabling, controlling, and codependent, and I'm likely to be told that my efforts to love and care for the addict and others in my family are *keeping us stuck in the problem*. I may also be told that I need to "get out of my disease" and to "pull back from all my unhealthy rescuing."

Caregiving Beyond Addiction

The primary focus of this book is on people who are in dependent relationships with an addict or alcoholic. However, the principles apply to almost any relationship—especially those in which one individual cares for and occasionally is called upon to "rescue" the other. This dynamic is readily apparent not just with addiction but also when dealing with chronic mental illness, chronic physical illnesses, war, trauma, and survivors of other similarly challenging issues. So, even though the focus of this work is on relationships affected by addiction, the principles behind it, those of prodependence, can and are meant to be extended to all such caregiving relationships.

THE STIGMA OF ADDICTION

Perhaps the difference in how we view caring for a loved one with a cancer diagnosis versus caring for an addicted loved one stems from the fact that addiction remains deeply stigmatized in our culture, viewed as a moral failing or a sign of inherent weakness. Our 1930s picture of the addict as a bum living in a shanty down by the river with no job, no family, and no future persists, even though only a very small percentage of addicts fit this stereotype.

Moreover, our perception of "addiction as a family disease" implies that everyone in an addict's family is pathologically unwell. Thus, the entire family is stigmatized by addiction, especially the person closest to the addict (most often the addict's spouse or a parent).

Despite everything we now know about addiction—what causes it, why some people are more susceptible than others, and how to treat it—addiction is viewed in nearly every culture (and in most families) as shameful, and silence is encouraged. Because of this, spouses, parents, and others who care for addicted loved ones tend to suffer in silence, providing care as best they can but with little or no useful guidance. There's too little information, there's too much shame, there's what the neighbors will say, etc. So families desperately work to "look good" on the outside while they collapse internally. When the problem is finally brought to light, the advice that loved ones often receive is to intervene and then detach and distance themselves from the problem. And woe to those who choose otherwise, as they will surely be blamed, shamed, and pathologized.

When these loving individuals do make their way to therapy, either on their own or in conjunction with the addict's treatment, do we honor and celebrate their devoted efforts at caregiving to the best of their ability and then offer them support and guidance? Hardly. Instead, we almost instantly assume they are enmeshed, enabling, controlling, and thus contributing to the problem. Then we give them a label—codependent—that sounds a lot like a diagnosis. Once labeled, these wounded, scared people are asked (at the height of a profound interpersonal crisis) to look at themselves and "their part" in the problem. They are told that they are ill, just like the addict, and they need to work on themselves so they can fix whatever it is they've been doing wrong.

How is this helpful? Why do we pin the stigma of addiction on the addict's family as well as the addict? Why do we negatively label hard-working, deeply loving, intensely loyal, profoundly afraid, nearly exhausted loved ones of addicts as codependent or worse? Is this the kindest and most effective way to invite them into the healing process? Does this represent the empathetic, nonjudgmental embrace that such people clearly need and deserve?

No wonder it's tough to keep family members of addicts involved in treatment. These are individuals who've spent months or even years trying to keep the family afloat, with hardly any thanks for their efforts, and now we're talking to them (or maybe at them) in ways that cause them to feel blamed, shamed, and at fault.

For years, I have listened to therapists and counselors talking about how difficult it is to work with the wives, husbands, and parents of addicts. I consistently hear statements like:

- They don't want to own up to their part in the problem.
- They view the addict as the sole source of the problem, and that makes it hard to help them.

- They don't see how their attempts to be caretakers are making things worse.
- They may be sober, but they're every bit as sick as the addicts, and sometimes sicker.
- They just can't stop rescuing, and that causes more problems than it solves.

Ouch!

LET'S TRY THIS ANOTHER WAY

What if loved ones of addicts aren't so difficult to treat? What if "the problem" lies more in how we conceptualize them? What if our primary model for treating them has misunderstood and marginalized them in ways that simultaneously confuse them and cause them to feel unnecessarily blamed and shamed? What if we prejudge loved ones of addicts as codependent, and therefore driving a dysfunctional family system? What if that "diagnosis" pushes them into a reactionary state where they feel they must defend their actions and tell us where the real problem lies, which, in their mind, is with the addict and we then go round and round with them, playing pin the tail on the pathology?

> What if loved ones of addicts aren't so difficult to treat? What if "the problem" lies more in how we conceptualize them? What if our primary model for treating them has misunderstood and marginalized them in ways that simultaneously confuse them and cause them to feel unnecessarily blamed and shamed?

I find it hard to understand why we choose to initiate therapeutic relationships with painfully overwhelmed and undersupported loved ones of addicts by thrusting a negative, pathological view of caregiving on them. Then we expect them to not only embrace this concept but to start working on it immediately. And when they act out against this model, we call them difficult, which reinforces our belief that they are as innately troubled as the addicts they love.

What about their grief for how their lives have turned out? What about their years of feeling confused, anxious, overwhelmed, and fearful about the future of their addicted loved one, themselves, and other members of their family? What about the fact that they have been victimized in their own homes, sometimes for years on end, by an addict who is more willing to lie, manipulate, and keep secrets than to face the truth?

Even when caregiving loved ones have been "doing it all wrong," experience has taught me that it's usually not a good idea to tell them that or to blame them in any way for facilitating and perpetuating someone else's dysfunction. And why would we expect otherwise? If you were exhausting yourself working part-time in three different places while taking care of multiple people, including an active addict, would you feel engaged by a message that asks you to start looking at *your problem*? Most likely you would not. Instead, this message would feel both hurtful and counterintuitive.

If our approach to loved ones of addicts alienates them before they can take advantage of the care and insight we can offer, then maybe we need to change our methodology. Maybe it's time to find a better, more empathetic and compassionate way to approach caregiving loved ones of addicts. Instead of blaming caregivers for resisting a path that feels innately wrong to them, maybe we should find a less intrusive, less shaming way of supporting them.

Twelve-Step Groups
for Loved Ones of Addicts

I fully endorse, encourage, and deeply believe in the meaningful support that programs like Al-Anon, ACoA, and CoDA offer to those fortunate enough to attend them. Having been a long-term participant in such environments, I'm forever grateful to the experience and the people in those rooms. To witness what occurs in those meetings is to witness prodependent healing in action. The peer support, shame reduction, and social bonding offered within such groups, combined with the shared language and perspective they create, can be immeasurably useful toward helping loved ones move past the fear and hopelessness wrought by active addiction. Such groups—day in and day out and absolutely free—provide both a structured process and a loving community to all those working toward the common goal of healing their family and their life.

That said, today I am more thoughtful about how and when I encourage caregiving loved ones to attend and participate in these groups. It is absolutely true that the faster we can get an addict into twelve-step recovery, the better, but for reasons discussed throughout this book, family members may not be ready for this type of support from day one, as they can interpret this suggestion as a sign that: (a) there is something wrong with them, or (b) they have been helping in the wrong way. In my experience, it is better to initially help family members by educating them about the nature of addiction and prodependence before encouraging them to go to any group where the potential messages might leave a novice attendee feeling at fault or blamed for the addict's problems.

EMPATHY: THE CORNERSTONE OF CONNECTION

The simple concept of an empathetic connection is well summed up by the oft-used social work phrase "be where the client is." This phrase means that, as therapists, we should closely track what clients are saying/doing/expressing/feeling and then reflect what we've heard. When we do this, our clients tend to feel safer and better understood. The simple act of being empathetic and curious about a client's experience, while simultaneously setting our own opinions and judgments aside, demonstrates in real time that we care about and want to understand the client's world.

So, no matter how distracted or out of touch we might get when working with someone in therapy—and hey, even good therapists have bad days—we can always refocus on the work at hand by directing ourselves back to what the person in front of us is expressing. This emphasis on understanding and continually reviewing the client's point of view and experience, no matter our own beliefs and feelings, is what keeps us in sync with and attentive to the work at hand.

In my experience, quick judgments (with a few important exceptions) are counterproductive to building a therapeutic alliance. This means my clients need to know me more as "the guy who leaves them feeling understood, safe, motivated, and hopeful" than as "the guy who points out what's wrong with them and pushes them to change." By demonstrating empathy and reflective compassion rather than assuming I understand the client as soon as he or she walks in the door and offering quick solutions based on that judgment, I earn the client's trust, and eventually the right to offer useful advice and direction. But I need to build that precious therapeutic alliance first. I need to be where the client is.

This means I don't verbalize my assumptions or ideas about how to help someone before that person has fully shown me, from his or her perspective, exactly what is needed. Until then, unless there is an emergency, I keep my ideas, suggestions, directions, beliefs, and assumptions to myself as I go about assessing, understanding, and relating to them. So, again, and I cannot state this any more clearly: The foundation of all useful therapeutic work is an empathetic, non-judgmental relationship where the client feels both understood and supported by the therapist.

Do I always agree with everything that every client says? No, I don't. And depending on the circumstances, I may, when the time is right, disclose what I think. If the timing is not right, I keep my thoughts to myself. Either way, if therapy and counseling are rooted in care and empathy for that person—demonstrated over and over by continually working to understand what that individual feels and believes—he or she will ultimately get what he or she came for. Without this respectful alliance, however, even the best therapeutic models and targeted advice are likely to fail. Unless and until someone seeking help feels my understanding and empathy for his or her lived experience, therapy doesn't work.

ADDICTS IN TREATMENT

Like everyone who seeks therapy, addicts need to be seen, heard, and responded to based on what they say, think, and feel. However, as therapists, we must also see, hear, and respond to an addict's *behavior* because, with active addicts, behavior is usually a much more accurate and honest indicator of where they really are and what they really need. We need to recognize that by the time addicts are troubled enough to seek help, their thoughts, feelings, and words are considerably less honest than the truths revealed by their actions.

Simply stated, active addicts are steeped in denial. They will insist, despite their addictive behavior patterns and the many consequences with which they are currently dealing, that they are doing just fine. They will say that they deeply love their spouse, kids, job, home, friends, etc., and would never do anything to jeopardize that. Yet when offered a chance to get high or act out with an addictive behavior, they will nearly always choose that path over a path that would protect the people, places, and things they profess to love and care about. Still, it's all under control as far as they are concerned.

What addicts tell a therapist (and everyone else in their lives) about what they feel, want, and need does not always align with their choices and behavior. Active addicts will say their goals are love and success, but they spend their time engaging in behaviors that are clearly out of sync with that. As therapists, we must recognize this and see through it. That is how we meet addicted clients where they are.

To reiterate, untreated addicts are out of control. By the time they get to therapy or treatment, their obsession with their drug or behavior of choice has pushed the arc of their lives askew. They are wobbling, out of balance, or worse. Therefore, meeting an addicted client where he or she is means we must trust what that person *does* more than what he or she *says*. Then we must help the addict see and accept the truth of the situation, while providing structure, containment, and accountability. Without this type of intervention, the addict will continue to live in harm's way. So, we must confront the addict's denial, challenge the addict's misguided thinking, and push the addict (sometimes kicking and screaming) toward sobriety and mental health.

LOVED ONES AND ADDICTION TREATMENT

As stated above, helping an active addict get and stay clean involves breaking through his or her denial while introducing containment, structure, guidance, support, and accountability (whether the addict wants it or not). But what about the needs of those who love the addict? How can we best support the spouse or family member of an addict? Do such people also need containment, structure, and accountability, or do their emotional needs differ from those of the addict? How do we meet such supportive loved ones where they are? And what do these often fearful, hurting, betrayed individuals need from therapy?

Nearly all the current books and treatments intended to help loved ones of addicts have been created by individuals focused on the ways in which childhood trauma can (and often does) affect adult relationships and life. The general thinking is that people who end up loving, partnering with, and staying with addicts are generally people who experienced similar trauma in childhood, usually by growing up with an alcoholic, addicted, or mentally ill parent or caregiver. Codependence in particular is focused on the belief that those who survive early-life dysfunction tend to carry that forward into their adult lives, often by bonding with and becoming dependent on people who, over time, neglect, abuse, and let them down in similar ways—thereby mirroring to some degree their past relationships, losses, and trauma.

This dynamic of re-creating childhood trauma by partnering with an addict likely makes perfect sense to those who've written about it as codependence because this is almost universally their lived experience. In fact, nearly all the major codependence literature, especially the earliest material, was written by women who say they experienced profound trauma in childhood, often related to an alcoholic father, only to grow up and re-create similar situations by marrying alcoholic men or becoming alcoholic and/or codependent themselves.[2]

Prodependence takes a vastly different approach, looking at addiction not from a trauma perspective but from an attachment perspective. Instead of viewing loved ones of addicts as inevitable victims of a traumatic past that has caught up with them and is now repeating itself in their adult lives—mostly in their relationship with the addict they're paired with—prodependence views them as valiant individuals struggling to love another person even in the face of addiction. With prodependence, there is no shame or blame, no sense of being wrong, no language that pathologizes the caregiving loved one. Instead, there is recognition for effort given, plus hope and useful instruction for healing.

Why, I ask, would we ever want to pathologize a person whose "problem" is typically defined as loving too much? Is loving too much even possible? If so, count me in. As a healthy friend, husband, and family member, my primary goal is to love all that I can love, to give all that I can give, and, if I am lucky enough, to be loved and cared for with the full heart and soul of the people who matter most in my life. Without a doubt, my love may at times be delivered in unskillful or ineffective ways. My love may get in the way of my own or others' healing without my seeing or knowing it. But please don't tell me that there is ever a time when I can love too much. Love poorly, yes. Love inadequately, yes. Love imperfectly, yes. Love in overly needful ways, yes. Love selfishly, yes. But love too much? No way.

Chapter Two

THE TIMES, THEY WERE A-CHANGING

Progress is impossible without change,
and those who cannot change their minds
cannot change anything.

—George Bernard Shaw

Before taking a deep dive into prodependence, the focus of this book, it's important to review the circumstances that evolved codependence. If we are to "move beyond codependency" in any meaningful way, as the subtitle of this book promises, we must first understand the origins of that model, along with the state of the psychotherapy and self-help worlds at the time the term was popularized. After all, codependence wasn't created in a vacuum. Its evolution was both a reflection of the times and a reaction to the personal experiences of those who created it.

From my perspective, five significant psychotherapeutic and cultural shifts preceded and fed the inception and development of codependence:

1) The emergence of humanistic psychology.
2) Psychotherapeutic and cultural recognition of the long-term effects of trauma.
3) The women's movement.
4) Development and implementation of the "disease model" of addiction.
5) Integration of systems theory into the disease model of addiction, leading to the "family disease" model of addiction.

HUMANISTIC PSYCHOLOGY

In the mid-twentieth century, the relatively static world of psychotherapy was rocked by a powerful and profound shift: humanistic psychology. Initially espoused by Carl Rogers, Abraham Maslow, and a few others, humanistic psychology addressed the many shortcomings of psychoanalytic theory (à la Sigmund Freud) and behaviorism (à la B. F. Skinner). Because humanistic psychology was such a clear departure from the practices espoused by Freud and Skinner, it was sometimes referred to as the "third force" in psychology.

Behavioral scientist Constance Fischer writes:

> Dissatisfactions with the 1950s partitive, deductive, and reductive experimental research model, with sterile and deterministic behaviorism, and with pathology-oriented psychoanalytic theory, led Abraham Maslow to form a mailing group of kindred professionals. He referred

to their efforts as the "third force" in psychology's evolution, following psychoanalysis and behaviorism. Their exchange of writings eventually grew into the *Journal of Humanistic Psychology* (founded in 1961).[1]

For the most part, humanistic psychology focuses on the idea of self-actualization, which is, essentially, the process of realizing one's full potential in life (being the best possible version of you that you can be). It encourages self-awareness and mindfulness as a way of changing one's thinking and behaviors. Part revelation, part revolution, humanistic psychology—focused more on ego-strength, self-awareness, and interpersonal relating than on individual pathology—offered therapists and clients a more holistic view of human potential than the determinist conclusions of behaviorism. At the same time, it relinquished the tightly imposed limitations of psychoanalysis.

This was, without a doubt, a freeing experience for both therapists and clients.

This new approach also appealed to countless thousands of seekers—people who were flocking to self-help programs and self-improvement seminars like EST, Lifespring, Insight, and Primal Scream, with each movement presenting a propriety mix of activities and exercises designed to help individuals self-actualize. These various attempts at seeking and self-actualization meshed with and mirrored other popular movements of the era, including Eastern philosophies, twelve-step recovery, and other support groups.

The shift in therapeutic culture wrought by humanistic psychology was (and remains) profound. Even the notoriously stodgy American Psychiatric Association was affected, with the organization's formerly staid annual conventions now hosting a variety of "sandal-footed, knap-sacked, openly breast-feeding members [who] interrupted symposium speakers from the audience with proclamations such as, 'I just have to tell you that I love your soul!'"[2]

Throughout the 1960s and '70s, riding a California-based wave of popular and clinical progressivism, master thinkers like Rodgers, Maslow, Rollo May, Irvin Yalom, Virginia Satir, and Viktor Frankl, among others, created and began to employ holistically humanist techniques like psychodrama, art therapy, intensive group therapy, family sculpting, equine-assisted psychotherapy, existential psychotherapy, and logotherapy, to name but a few. All of which were intended to switch the therapeutic focus from pathology, years of introspection on the couch, and intellectual efforts at behavioral control to self-development, self-esteem, creativity, and informed choice.

The tenets of humanistic psychology are perhaps best summarized by Tom Greening in the *Journal of Humanistic Psychology.*

- Human beings, as human, supersede the sum of their parts. They cannot be reduced to components.
- Human beings have their existence in a uniquely human context, as well as in a cosmic ecology.
- Human beings are aware and are aware of being aware—i.e., they are conscious. Human consciousness always includes an awareness of oneself in the context of other people.
- Human beings have the ability to make choices and therefore have responsibility.
- Human beings are intentional, aim at goals, are aware that they cause future events, and seek meaning, value, and creativity.[3]

Pretty trippy, huh? Needless to say, this perspective was a sea-change from the stuffy, relatively nonrelational psychoanalytic and behaviorist movements that preceded it.

RECOGNITION OF TRAUMA

As the humanistic psychology movement was gaining steam, we were also looking at the concept of trauma. Prior to this era, traumatized individuals, when they manifested symptoms of trauma and sought help to understand their feelings, were most often "diagnosed" as weak-willed and inherently emotionally unhealthy. Only rarely did treatment consider the impact of their potentially overwhelming life experiences. Instead, we tended to look at their trauma symptoms and focus on one or more of the following:

- Identifying and treating their underlying pathology, whatever that was deemed to be—essentially telling them, "You're a mess (whether you know it or not), and that's the reason you think, react, and behave this way."
- Strengthening their psychological mettle—essentially telling them, "Pull yourself up by your bootstraps."
- Coaching them to suppress past traumas to keep them from interfering with the present, often using techniques (including medications) designed to block trauma symptoms.

Therapists of the era had little to no training in or understanding of trauma and its wide-ranging, long-lasting effects, so they mostly avoided the issue, providing neither resolution nor hope.

The trauma field took a big leap forward in the late 1960s as war-hardened Vietnam veterans returned home, manifesting multiple profound emotional, psychological, and behavioral problems—including addiction. The impact of the war on these men was significant and undeniable. They went to Vietnam healthy and whole;

they returned from the war beaten and broken. And it wasn't just the soldiers who identified this change, their friends and families also noticed a huge difference.

Importantly, these men could not be dismissed by psychologists as "hysterical weaklings," as we'd done with trauma survivors in the past. Because of this, we finally took a serious look at the ways in which past traumas can impact a person's current thinking and behavior—an idea that immediately resonated with both mental health professionals and people who'd experienced severe trauma, including people who'd never served in the military or been anywhere near a battlefield.

Recognizing this, scholars like Christine Courtois, Bessel van der Kolk, and John Briere asked, "Can the symptoms we see with combat veterans also manifest in the general population in response to other forms of trauma?" The answer was an undeniable yes. The research that they and others conducted made it clear that trauma as seen in Vietnam veterans is no different, in terms of later-life manifestations, than trauma experienced by victims of sexual abuse, domestic violence, racial intolerance, homophobia, gender discrimination, violent crime, misogyny, bullying, neglect, chronic family dysfunction (including alcoholism and mental illness), etc.

In 1980, the American Psychiatric Association responded to this research by adding its first trauma-focused diagnosis, post-traumatic stress disorder (PTSD). The new diagnosis identified three primary symptoms:

1) Reexperiencing trauma—in flashbacks, nightmares, and even in response to loud noises and stressful situations.
2) Numbed response as a way of coping with the pain of re-experiencing.

3) Hypervigilance—anxiety, psychological arousal, jumpiness, overreactions, etc.

The arrival of PTSD as an official diagnosis dovetailed nicely with the rapidly evolving clinical views of humanistic psychology, where individuals were looked at holistically, with each facet of a person's life seen as impacting other aspects of his or her life.

In her writings, Courtois defines trauma as "any event or experience (including witnessing) that is physically and/or psychologically overwhelming to the exposed individual."[4] She also states that trauma has both objective and subjective dimensions, meaning trauma "can involve just about any type of adversity or harm, and a person's response is dependent on his or her individualized experience, perspective, and temperament."[5] In other words, people can react very differently to the same situation. For instance, a new mother with her infant child in the car would likely be more profoundly traumatized by a fender bender than a professional race car driver.

My point here is that starting in the late 1960s, we began to explore and understand the now well-accepted idea that trauma, no matter how it occurs, can have both immediate and long-lasting effects, such as:

- Flashbacks
- Nightmares
- Anxiety
- Depression
- Stress
- Shame
- Lowered self-esteem

- Inability to develop and maintain emotional intimacy
- Physical illness
- Rage/violence
- Addiction

In today's world, we readily acknowledge the link between early-life trauma and numerous later-life symptoms and disorders. An immense amount of research has confirmed this link. One study looking at the long-term effects of unresolved early-life trauma found that survivors are:

- 1.8 times as likely to smoke cigarettes
- 1.9 times as likely to become obese
- 2.4 times as likely to experience ongoing anxiety
- 3.6 times as likely to be depressed
- 3.6 times as likely to qualify as promiscuous
- 7.2 times as likely to become alcoholic
- 11.1 times as likely to become an intravenous drug user[6]

As therapeutic recognition of trauma grew through the 1970s and into the 1980s, so did public acceptance. Laws were enacted to protect children and spouses from abuse in the home, rape and domestic violence crisis centers popped up in major cities, and hotlines were created to help suicidal individuals find much-needed immediate assistance. In conjunction with this, frank conversations about trauma and trauma-related issues took place in small groups and on a cultural scale, making it less shameful to need and ask for help. In particular, John Bradshaw's PBS programs discussing shame and the wounded inner-child brought the dynamics of addicted families and trauma into the light.

Dysfunction Gets Trendy

By the early 1980s, the once deeply personal and private stories of addiction and emotional trauma (the long-hidden realities of mental illness, addiction, and profound family dysfunction) burst on the public scene in a big way. Once out of the closet, such issues almost immediately became powerful fodder for pop culture entertainment, delivered to the masses in the form of daytime television talk shows. Starting then and still going strong today, the painful face of real human tragedy has provided trendy viewing candy. Why watch the manufactured pain of actors in soap opera scripts—the other popular form of daytime televised entertainment—when you could suddenly watch real people's real pain play out in real time? These formerly private discussions, suddenly made public, turned many a TV personality into a name brand—Phil Donahue, Sally Jessy Raphael, Dr. Phil, Dr. Drew, Oprah, and many others.

As the trauma movement grew, therapists began to look at family-wide issues wrought by global traumas, such as how addiction and mental illness affect everyone close to the addict. About this dynamic, John Bradshaw writes:

Family secrets can go back for generations. They can be about suicides, homicides, incest, abortions, addictions, public loss of face, financial disaster, etc. All the secrets get acted out. This is the power of toxic shame. The pain and suffering of shame generate automatic and unconscious defenses. Freud called these defenses by various names:

denial, idealization of parents, repression of emotions, and dissociation from emotions. What is important to note is that we can't know what we don't know. Denial, idealization, repression, and dissociation are unconscious survival mechanisms. Because they are unconscious, we lose touch with the shame, hurt, and pain they cover up. We cannot heal what we cannot feel. So without recovery, our toxic shame gets carried for generations.[7]

This is the basic idea of trauma. It happens to us, and it happens to those we love. And if we don't find a way to recognize it, call it out, and find better ways to cope with it, it will color our thinking and behavior indefinitely.

THE WOMEN'S MOVEMENT

The 1960s, 1970s, and early 1980s brought upheaval, not just to the world of therapy, but to the world at large. One major area of social change that likely had a direct influence on the codependence movement was the women's rights movement.

By the early 1960s, women all around the United States and the world were growing increasingly frustrated with and vocal about the cultural and legal limitations placed on their social and economic status. As women were striving to have their voices heard in a man's world, they often embraced traditionally male traits like focusing on winning as opposed to community building, achievement as opposed to empathy, and always being right (even when they weren't). Their goal was to beat men at their own game. To this end, they understandably shed, devalued, or placed on the back burner a few traditionally female values and strengths, such as compassion, mutuality, and working together to make the family/community/world a better place.

Whatever routes they took, women were right to push for change. Let's face it, for centuries they'd been viewed as "the weaker sex," and their most socially acceptable role (maybe their only socially acceptable role) was wife and mother—barefoot, pregnant, and in the kitchen. When Betty Friedan's wildly controversial (at the time) book, *The Feminine Mystique*, was published in 1963, the majority of women got married in their early twenties, few women attended college, and 60 percent of the women who did attend college dropped out to get married.[8] As Friedan eloquently pointed out, a woman's ambitions outside the home, if she dared to have them, were more likely to be denigrated and thwarted (by society and a legal system that treated women as second-class citizens) than supported.

Enough was enough. Women were tired of these anachronistic standards. In short order, support for the Equal Rights Amendment (initially introduced in Congress in 1921) resurfaced. In 1971, the House and Senate overwhelmingly approved an updated version of the ERA (354–24 in the House, 84–8 in the Senate). The proposed amendment was then presented to the states for approval, with a ratification deadline of March 22, 1979. By the end of 1977, the amendment had been ratified by thirty-five of the necessary thirty-eight states and enactment seemed inevitable—until antifeminist activist Phyllis Schlafly mobilized conservatives and argued (speciously but nonetheless effectively) that the amendment would be bad for housewives and would cause women to be drafted into the military (even though the amendment specifically stated that women would be exempt from the draft). With this, the equal rights movement stalled, and feminist voices were once again trampled.

Nevertheless, women carried the message of the times—that men and women are equal—into the workplace and beyond, continuing in their efforts to be more assertive and gain equality.

Think about the wonderfully entertaining movie *9 to 5*, starring Lily Tomlin, Dolly Parton, and Jane Fonda. In this film, three female employees working for a sexist, lying, hypocritical male bigot turn the tables and take control of their workplace (committing about a hundred very funny felonies in the process). The movie hit the big screen in 1980, and much of its appeal centered around its timely feminist theme. In fact, this "girl power" film nicely represents, though in a somewhat twisted way, the progressive steps forward that women were trying to take and the ways in which they were going about it—primarily by one-upping their male boss and beating him at his own game.

The fact that so many women identified with the plot of *9 to 5* is an indication of just how profoundly disempowered women of the era truly were. And the film very clearly illustrates that the women of that era determined that the best way to get ahead likely sounded something like this: "If you want to succeed in a man's world, act more like a man!" If getting ahead meant being more assertive and less emotionally generous, or less empathic and more direct, so be it. Thus, on nearly every level, women were making a very conscious effort to be *less dependent* on men (for self-esteem, income, survival, happiness, etc.), with a much greater focus on independence.

Melody Beattie laid this out almost perfectly in *Codependent No More* when she stated:

> Stop centering and focusing on other people. Settle down with and in ourselves. Stop seeking so much approval and validation from others.

We don't need the approval of everyone and anyone. We only need our approval. We have all the same sources for happiness and making choices inside us that others do. Find and develop our own internal supply of peace, well-being, and self-esteem. Relationships help, but they cannot be our source. Develop personal cores of emotional security with ourselves.[9]

Do you think this message, way back in the 1980s, was crafted for both sexes? Do you think this message appealed to both sexes? I don't. And here is why: Men were already acting under these assumptions. The statement above could, in fact, be a one-paragraph primer on how to act more like a man and less like a woman.

The message of codependency took root quickly because women in the 1970s and '80s demanding equality in male-dominated workplaces that had nearly always viewed them as second-class citizens was a tall order. There were a whole lot of glass ceilings yet to be broken. So, when people ask me, "What do you think made the concept of codependency into the sensation it was during that period?" my answer nearly always relates to this specific issue. We were living in a time where newly liberated women wanted their fair share. Thus, codependency, with clearly articulated anti-dependency messages like the one from Beattie, was in.

THE DISEASE MODEL OF ADDICTION

Amidst all this therapeutic and social upheaval, we were also rethinking addiction. Prior to this, addiction had traditionally been defined by both professionals and the public as a moral failing, a lack of self-will, or a deep psychological flaw (personality disorder) rather than a chronic form of emotional illness. This moralistic belief system was prevalent until the mid-twentieth century, when our understanding and view of addiction began to slowly but steadily shift.

A trio of groups—the Research Council on Problems of Alcohol (RCPA), the Yale Center of Alcohol Studies, and the National Committee for Education on Alcoholism—were leaders in switching focus in the addiction conversation onto the *disease* of alcoholism and addiction, rather than the inherent evils of alcohol and drugs and the moral failings of people who get hooked on them. In 1942, Dwight Anderson of the RCPA proposed a quartet of "kinetic ideas" regarding alcoholism:

1) The problem drinker is a sick man, exceptionally reactive to alcohol.
2) He can be helped.
3) He is worth helping.
4) The problem is therefore a responsibility of the healing professions as well as health authorities and the public.[10]

Two years later, Marty Mann, the first woman to get sober as a member of Alcoholics Anonymous, added a fifth tenet to Anderson's work.

5) Alcoholism is a disease.[11]

Soon thereafter, the "Minnesota Model" of viewing and treating alcoholism as a disease rather than a moral failing took root. Pioneer House, Hazelden, and Willmar State Hospital, all located in Minnesota, implemented programs (heavily based on the experience of sober members of Alcoholics Anonymous) in 1948, 1949, and 1950 respectively. These treatment centers viewed alcoholism as a primary disorder (rather than a symptom of some other psychological disorder) best treated with long-term abstinence and sobriety-focused social support.[12]

Part and parcel with implementation of the disease model was recognition that *addicts are often survivors of severe or chronic trauma.*[13] And the more we know about addiction, the more sense this makes. It is clear from both research and clinical observation that addictions are not about *feeling good*, they're about *feeling less.* Addicts turn to addictive substances and behaviors not because they want to have a good time, but to self-medicate and self-regulate their emotions. Their primary goal is to *escape from life* and to *not feel* stress, anxiety, depression, fear, and other forms of discomfort.

> It is clear from both research and clinical observation that addictions are not about *feeling good,* they're about *feeling less.* Addicts turn to addictive substances and behaviors not because they want to have a good time, but to self-medicate and self-regulate their emotions.

And don't kid yourself, addiction works if your goal is to escape reality. Addictive substances and behaviors trigger a *highly distracting* neurochemical response—primarily the release of dopamine (pleasure), along with adrenaline (excitement), oxytocin (love and connection), serotonin (emotional well-being), and a variety of endorphins (euphoria). This response creates sensations of pleasure, excitement, control, and, most important, *distraction and emotional/psychological escape.*

Addicts abuse addictive substances and behaviors not to feel better, but to escape. And they continue to do so even as their clearly (to an external observer) out-of-control behavior creates significant problems: relationship issues, trouble at work or in school, declining physical and/or emotional health, financial turmoil, legal concerns, mood disorders, and more. Addicts cope with stress, depression, anxiety, loneliness, boredom, attachment deficits, and unresolved trauma by getting high instead of turning to other people who might emotionally support them. As they do this repeatedly, their choice becomes a pattern and then an addiction. As Gabor Maté writes in his bestselling book, *In the Realm of Hungry Ghosts*, "It is impossible to understand addiction without asking what relief the addict finds, or hopes to find, in the drug or the addictive behavior."[14]

By the mid-1980s, the disease model and our understanding of trauma merged into a single model of understanding and treating addiction. This model, as I see it, can be summarized as follows:

> Addicts are almost universally traumatized as children (or sometimes later in life), which affects their ability to attach in healthy ways. Thus, they learn to use fantasy and dissociation via substances and behaviors for emotional regulation, rather than relying on intimate family, friends, and community for emotional support as a healthier person might. In time, they become compulsive and obsessed with this substance or behavior, using it as their primary emotional and psychological coping mechanism.

As stated earlier, addictions are not about pleasure. Instead, they're about the secondary gain of escape. Nonaddicted people drink, use drugs, and engage in potentially addictive behaviors because these things are, first and foremost, pleasurable. For nonaddicts, pleasure is the primary gain. Not so for addicts. Addicts may pretend to themselves (and others) that they are using to have fun, but in reality they're more interested in the secondary gain of escape. A healthy, nonaddicted person drinks a martini to get a little high, to relax, and to enjoy life. An addict drinks half a dozen martinis to escape the world and everything in it. And the addict goes back for more of the same, day after day, seeking and finding this same secondary gain, eventually getting stuck in an endless loop of feeling bad, drinking to escape that feeling, and then feeling bad again—possibly worse than before because of the regrettable things he or she did while drunk, which leads to more drinking.

That is the cycle of addiction.

Today, both the disease model and the role of trauma, especially unresolved early-life trauma, in the etiology of addiction are well accepted. As Maté writes, "A hurt is at the center of all addictive behaviors. It is present in the gambler, the internet addict, the compulsive shopper, and the workaholic."[15] This means that addictions form because trauma has poisoned the well of interpersonal attachment. Thanks to unresolved early-life trauma, addicts learn to associate fear rather than comfort to deep human intimacy and attachment. Thus, they refuse to turn to others, even loved ones, for help when they're struggling or feeling down. Instead, they compulsively and obsessively self-soothe by numbing out with addictive substances and behaviors.

SYSTEMS THEORY AND THE "FAMILY DISEASE" OF ADDICTION

Implementation of the disease model of addiction was, in most respects, a wonderful thing. Addicts were no longer vilified as bums and losers, and we finally had a useful, nonmoralistic medical model to implement when treating them.

Unfortunately, family systems theory, which thinks about the family as a conglomeration of interrelated parts, got pulled into the disease model of addiction in ways that have, over time, been unhelpful to loved ones of addicts. When systems theory got applied to the disease model of addiction, our thinking shifted from looking at the alcoholic alone to looking at the addict's entire family as a pathological system. Suddenly, everyone in the family was seen as playing a meaningful and pathological role in the formation and maintenance of addiction. We went from focusing on the disease of the addict to focusing on the disease of the entire family.

> When systems theory got applied to the disease model of addiction, our thinking shifted from looking at the alcoholic alone to looking at the addict's entire family as a pathological system. Suddenly, everyone in the family was seen as playing a meaningful and pathological role in the formation and maintenance of addiction.

But what was this "family disease"? With addicts, the primary manifestation of the disease of addiction was obviously their obsession with their drug or behavior of choice. With family members, things weren't so clear. The general thinking seemed to be that if the addict's disease centered on obsession, so did the family's, so therapists decided to view the family's disease as an obsession, not with the addictive substance, but with the addict and his or her addiction-driven behavior.

As the 1980s progressed, partners and other loved ones of addicts were increasingly viewed as contributing (and even integral) to the formation and maintenance of addiction. And the family's enabling, fixing, controlling, and rescuing behaviors, sometimes to their own or the addict's detriment, could now be explained as an unhealthy obsession with the addict and his or her behavior.

That said, early research on the family dynamics of addiction was split into two distinct branches:

1) The impact of addiction on individual family members— viewing family members as adaptive survivors of an addictive process.

2) The impact of individual family members on the addiction— viewing family members as factors driving the addiction.

The first path, to me, was very much on target, as it recognized loved ones of addicts as the traumatized individuals they are. This path also recognized that the addict's highly dysfunctional, sometimes abusive, addiction-driven behaviors are often the primary source of the family's immediate pain and trauma. The second path is where I think we went awry. With this path, the onus of addiction was pushed onto "enmeshed, enabling, and controlling" family members as much as on the addict and his or her underlying trauma.[16]

Unfortunately, the second path is the one the addiction field seemed to grab onto. Because of this, as the disease model of addiction came into vogue, so did the blaming and shaming of family members, especially wives. Wives of addicts were routinely viewed, judged, and labeled as psychologically unhealthy women who chose men predisposed toward addiction (for one reason or another) and then pushed them over the edge.

About this thinking, addiction historian William White writes:

> The general profile of the alcoholic wife depicted in this early literature was that of a woman who was neurotic, sexually repressed, dependent, man-hating, domineering, mothering, guilty and masochistic, and/or hostile and nagging. The typical therapist's view of the wife of the alcoholic was generally one of "I'd drink, too, if I were married to her."[17]

My point here is that addiction was increasingly viewed as a family disease rather than a disease afflicting only the addict. And family members, especially wives, were increasingly characterized as causative factors in the addiction rather than as adaptive survivors. Basically, the family's "obsession with the addict" was viewed through the same lens as the addict's "obsession with the drug."

Chapter Three

A BRIEF EXAMINATION OF CODEPENDENCE

Codependence: A psychological condition or a relationship in which a person is controlled or manipulated by another who is affected with a pathological condition (such as an addiction to alcohol or heroin); broadly: dependence on the needs of or control by another.[1]

—Merriam-Webster

odependence, as commonly understood, occurs when one person tries to control the actions of another (in the guise of helping) so that he or she can feel better about himself or herself and his or her relationship with that other person. The codependence model is rooted in discussions of early life trauma and the ways in which that can affect later life behaviors and relationships. Unfortunately, for many loved ones of addicts (and plenty of therapists), framing a person's commitment to helping a troubled loved one as stemming from that person's reignited early life trauma (as opposed to being an expression of love and commitment) feels negative, as if the caregiving loved one is being blamed, shamed, and pejoratively labeled for loving too much, or not in the right way, or for selfish reasons.

This was likely not the original intent of the codependence movement, but it's what we've currently got. The movement's progenitors were almost certainly not trying to say that loved ones of addicts provide care based solely on their personal insecurities and neuroses. The originators of codependence did, however, notice that most of the people in meaningful relationships with an addict had chaotic and traumatic pasts. And this observation was carried forward as a primary tenet of the codependence model, which in turn led to many people feeling blamed, shamed, and wrongly pathologized.

THE INCEPTION OF CODEPENDENCE

The word *codependence* did not come into vogue until the 1980s, but the ideas took root several decades earlier. The true beginnings likely occurred in 1941 with German-born psychoanalyst Karen Horney's theory of the "moving toward" personality style, where one person subconsciously tries to control another through seemingly unselfish, virtuous, faithful, and martyr-like behavior.[2]

A decade later, in 1951, a support group for loved ones of alcoholics, Al-Anon, was founded, recognizing, among other things, the role of "moving toward" behaviors in perpetuating the disease of addiction.[3] Al-Anon addressed, for the first time, the flip-side of the alcoholism equation: the pain experienced by the long-suffering spouses and families of alcoholics—the struggles of the people who felt overwhelmed by, at the mercy of, and obsessed with managing their loved one's drinking.

By the 1970s, therapists and drug and alcohol treatment centers had embraced the Al-Anon model, recognizing that addictions affect not only the addict but the addict's family. In 1979, *Newsweek* published an article by Dr. Claudia Black, Dr. Stephanie Brown, and Sharon Wegscheider (now Wegscheider-Cruse) about adult children of alcoholics, introducing to the public the idea that alcoholism in a family can and does cause lifelong patterns of dysfunctional behavior for all members of the family, even those who never take a drink.[4] With this, popular culture embraced the therapeutic belief in treating the disease of addiction not just individually but as part of a family system, and spouses were suddenly referred to as *co-alcoholic, co-addict,* or *co-chemically dependent,* labels that were eventually consolidated and shortened into the much catchier term, *codependent.*

The word codependent, in addition to being memorable, removed the terms alcoholic, addict, and chemically dependent from the "co" label. This sanitized the label for family members who weren't addicted and did not want, even inadvertently, to be labeled as such. It also extended the reach of codependency to anyone in an overly dependent relationship, with or without the presence of addiction. The term's originally intended link to another person's active pathology (most often addiction) was lost. Suddenly, you could have this problem with or without an addict in your life. You could be a "co" all on your own.

By the late 1980s, primarily with the release of six books, the term codependence and the ideas surrounding it entered the layperson's lexicon.

- In 1981 Claudia Black wrote, *It Will Never Happen to Me: Children of Alcoholics as Youngsters, Adolescents, Adults.*[5]
- In 1982, Janet Woititz wrote *Adult Children of Alcoholics.*[6]
- In 1985, Robin Norwood wrote *Women Who Love Too Much: When You Keep Wishing and Hoping He'll Change.*[7]
- In 1986, Timmen Cermak wrote *Diagnosing and Treating Co-dependence.*[8]
- In 1986, Melody Beattie wrote *Codependent No More: How to Stop Controlling Others and Start Caring for Yourself.*[9]
- In 1989, Pia Mellody wrote *Facing Codependence: What It Is, Where It Comes From, How It Sabotages Our Lives.*[10]

In *Codependent No More*, Beattie identifies and addresses the pseudo-pathology that has long been attached to the codependence model, writing, "Perhaps one reason some professionals call co-dependency a disease is because many codependents are reacting to an illness such as alcoholism."[11] There is much impact in this statement. First, it indicates (in my opinion) that Beattie never intended for codependency to be a pathology, that she was instead focused on gaining insight into the partner's experience. Next, it shows she realized, right from the start, that a lot of people would nonetheless view codependence as pathology. So, even before codependence became *a thing* in the collective mindset, Beattie sensed it would be tied to the disease model of addiction, in particular the belief that addiction is a family illness.

Timmen Cermak espoused this opinion rather forcefully, even proposing an official psychiatric diagnosis for codependence. Cermak's suggested criteria included behaviors such as:

- Enmeshment in relationships with other psychologically unhealthy people
- Boundary distortions around intimacy
- Meeting other people's needs to the exclusion of one's own needs
- Tying one's self-esteem to validation and support from others
- Anxiety and hypervigilance about relationships and potential separation
- Depression
- Denial of situational reality
- A history of trauma[12]

Ultimately, Cermak's proposed codependency diagnosis was rejected by the American Psychiatric Association, but the codependency books and terminology stuck around, resonating in various ways with loved ones of addicts and leading to the formation of a new twelve-step fellowship, Co-Dependents Anonymous (CoDA), with its first meeting October 22, 1986.[13]

One of the better explanations of the early codependency movement appears in the foreword of Pia Mellody's book, *Facing Codependence*. There, Andrea Wells Miller and J. Keith Miller write:

It was actually the families of alcoholics and other chemically dependent people who brought [codependency] to the attention of therapists in treatment centers. These family members all seemed to be plagued with intensified feelings of shame, fear, anger, and pain in their relationships with the alcoholic or addict who was the focal point of their family. But they often were not able to express these feelings in a healthy way because of a compulsion to please and care for the addicted person. . . . One irrational aspect was that most of the family members had a deluded hope that if they could only be perfect in their "relating to" and "help-ing" the alcoholic, he or she would become sober—and they, the family members, would be free of their awful shame, pain, fear, and anger.[14]

This statement recognizes and summarizes the feelings that many loved ones of addicts say they experience when dealing with addicted family members. They mistakenly think, "If I can just control the other person's addiction in some way, everything will turn out the way that I'd like."

Based on this, codependence literature has come to identify co-dependent people as men and women who are overly affected by someone else's behavior, or men and women who are overly focused on controlling someone else's behavior. Moreover, the belief of the codependence movement is that rescuing an addicted loved one is not as benevolent as it might at first glance appear because solving another person's problems when they should really be addressing those problems themselves prevents growth in them. Thus, caretak-ing in this "rescuer" sense is counterproductive and may, in a way, victimize the person who is being helped.

Based on this belief, the advice typically given by codependence writers and therapists is that it's better for loved ones of addicts to detach and focus on caring for themselves—in particular, working to heal their own assumed trauma (the trauma that is said to under-lie and drive their unhealthy caretaking)—than to focus on their troubled loved one. Beattie writes in *Codependent No More*, "Detach. Detach in love, detach in anger, but strive for detachment. I know it's difficult, but it will become easier with practice. If you can't let go completely, try to 'hang on loose.' Relax. Sit back. Now, take a deep breath. The focus in on you."[15] More than three decades later, this advice, though in a somewhat altered and more strident form, is still given by addiction therapists and members of CoDA.

WHY CODEPENDENCE STRUCK A CHORD

The codependence movement, once introduced, took off like a rocket. One reason for this was that it was the first readily accessible theory addressing the impact of addiction on the family. It identified addiction-driven family dysfunction as the powerful and profoundly impactful trauma that it is, and a whole lot of people identified with that. With codependence, family members of addicts could finally view themselves, their feelings, and their behaviors through a lens that recognized and accepted the emotional effects of their loved one's addiction.

Moreover, like the self-actualization and women's rights movements that preceded it, codependence encouraged women to empower themselves by focusing on themselves and their needs first, while setting better boundaries with the men in their lives. The message for women in relationship with addicted men was that instead of giving themselves fully to the addict and attempts to manage and control the addiction (and the addict), they should examine their own needs, engage in self-care, and set healthy boundaries with the addict and others in their lives. In short, women were encouraged to love and care for themselves as well as for their addicted husbands.

This new approach to relating gave women permission to differentiate as individuals—to take control of their own lives while simultaneously releasing control over their addicted loved ones. To a 1980s nation of women eager for equality, this message was like mother's milk. The idea was both empowering and easily embraced.

CONFLATION WITH A GENUINE PATHOLOGY (DEPENDENT PERSONALITY DISORDER)

Right from the start, codependence was conflated with a long established psychological disorder, Dependent Personality Disorder (DPD). DPD is characterized by "a pervasive and excessive need to be taken care of that leads to submissive and clinging behavior and fears of separation, beginning by early adulthood and present in a variety of contexts."[16] For a DPD diagnosis, individuals must display five or more of the following criteria:

- Difficulty making everyday decisions without an excessive amount of advice and reassurance.
- Needing others to assume responsibility for most major areas of life.
- Difficulty expressing disagreement (based on fear of rejection and loss of support).
- Difficulty initiating projects or doing things on one's own.
- Going to excessive lengths to obtain nurturance and support from others, to the point of volunteering to do things that are unpleasant.
- Feeling uncomfortable or helpless when alone.
- Urgently seeking a new relationship as a source of care and support when one relationship ends.
- An unrealistic preoccupation with the fear of being left alone to take care of oneself.[17]

This diagnosis sounds a lot like Timmen Cermak's proposed co-dependency diagnosis discussed earlier in this chapter, which could be a primary reason Cermak's proposal was rejected. The American Psychiatric Association may have felt that people who take enmeshment and attempts to influence or control the behavior of others to an extreme were already covered by the DPD diagnosis.

CODEPENDENCE GONE AWRY

Unfortunately, the concept of codependence quickly morphed—in the minds of the public, a large segment of the therapeutic community, and many of the people who self-label as codependent—into an unofficial pathology (that sounds a lot like Dependent Personality Disorder), rather than a relatively normal response to an abnormal situation (the trauma wrought by a loved one's addiction). This morphed viewpoint is now so pervasive that if you go to the Wikipedia page for Dependent Personality Disorder and scroll to the "See Also" section at the bottom, the first hyperlink is to Wikipedia's page on codependency—tangible evidence of how closely aligned the two terms have become in the public mind.[18]

Beattie, perhaps inadvertently, feeds this belief in *Codependent No More*, writing:

> When a codependent discontinued his or her relationship with a troubled person, the codependent frequently sought another troubled person and repeated the codependent behaviors with that new person. These behaviors, or coping mechanisms, seemed to prevail throughout the codependent's life—if that person didn't change these behaviors.[19]

So, intentionally or otherwise, codependency now applies a pathological sheen to those who love and care for addicts. It's like the world woke up one day and decided that displays of inherently powerful and traditionally feminine strengths like compassion, empathy, and caregiving were somehow a step backward. And based on that, both genders were taught, through the language of codependence, that if you let someone else's needs meaningfully guide your actions, you are weak, and you are never going to succeed.

That is not codependence. It's antidependence.

As stated earlier, this was likely not the intention of the codependency movement's progenitors. Nevertheless, caring for an addicted loved one was slowly but steadily pathologized—if not officially, then in the collective mindset. In time, codependence came to mean caring for yourself *instead of* your addicted loved one rather than caring for yourself *as well as* your addicted loved one (as the co-addiction movement originally intended and encouraged).

> In time, codependence came to mean caring for yourself *instead of* your addicted loved one, rather than caring for yourself *as well as* your addicted loved one (as the co-addiction movement originally intended and encouraged).

Nowadays, people labeled as codependent are often treated as if they have Dependent Personality Disorder, even when their behavior does not even remotely approach that level of pathological neediness and enmeshment. Ross Rosenberg, author of *The Human Magnet Syndrome*,[20] discusses this unfortunate transition in a Psych Central article:

> Like other misunderstood and misused psychological expressions, "codependency" has taken on a life of its own. Once it went mainstream, it was haphazardly and conveniently reshaped to fit our mainstream vocabulary. Since its introduction in the 1980s, its meaning has devolved to describe a weak, needy, clingy, and even emotionally sick person.[21]

Rosenberg's statement may seem harsh, but it's absolutely on target. Codependence has evolved into a belief system that says caring for and trying to help another person, especially if that person is addicted, is, in and of itself, an unhealthy, dysfunctional, possibly pathological behavior. Consider the following statement by counselor Scott Egleston, as quoted in *Codependent No More*: "Codependents are caretakers—rescuers. They rescue, then they persecute, then they end up victimized."[22]

That sounds like an accusation of pathology to me, or at least a manifestation of the pathological interpersonal dysfunction described in the Karpman Drama Triangle.

The Karpman Drama Triangle

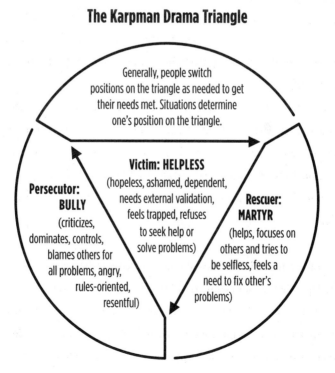

Generally, people switch positions on the triangle as needed to get their needs met. Situations determine one's position on the triangle.

Victim: HELPLESS
(hopeless, ashamed, dependent, needs external validation, feels trapped, refuses to seek help or solve problems)

Persecutor: BULLY
(criticizes, dominates, controls, blames others for all problems, angry, rules-oriented, resentful)

Rescuer: MARTYR
(helps, focuses on others and tries to be selfless, feels a need to fix other's problems)

About the codependency-drama interaction, Beattie says:

> We rescue "victims"—people who we believe are not capable of being responsible for themselves. . . . After we rescue, we will inevitably move to the next corner of the triangle: persecution. We become resentful and angry at the person we have so generously 'helped.' . . . Then it's time for our final move. We head right for our favorite spot: the victim corner on the *bottom*. This is the predictable and unavoidable result of a rescue. Feelings of helplessness, hurt, sorrow, shame, and self-pity abound. We have been used—again. We have gone unappreciated—again. . . . We wonder, shall we forever be victims? Probably, if we don't stop rescuing.[23]

So, according to the codependence model, the answer to one's problems is to stop rescuing. No rescue, no drama. If loved ones of addicts will just look within to identify the true source of their pathological rescuing (their unresolved trauma), they will be able to detach with love, to stop caretaking, and to stop creating drama. Or so the theory goes.

To this end, spouses, parents, siblings, and friends of addicts are routinely counseled to accept their own trauma-based weakness, to step away from the dysfunctional relationship, to stop rescuing, to stop enabling, to detach with love, and to "stop being so codependent." Unfortunately, this approach does not empathetically meet them where they are (anxious, fearful, angry, etc.). Because of that, they often respond negatively to these suggestions, thinking and saying things like, "How can I possibly abandon a person I love, especially in his or her hour of deepest need?"

And therein lies the problem. Codependency as a model does not meet loved ones of addicts where they are. Instead, it prejudges them, and then, based on that prejudgment, it tells them what to do. As a result, confused, overwhelmed, needful loved ones of addicts take away messages like:

- I am an active part of the problem.
- Caring for my addicted loved one has made things worse.
- I am broken and defective and unworthy of a healthier relationship.
- I should have seen this coming.
- I don't know how to love someone.

Still, family members, friends, pastors, and, yes, even well-educated therapists will work to convince a person who loves and cares for an addict that trying to help that individual, a person they've been close to for a very long time (maybe their entire life), is irrational and counterproductive and a sign of their own dysfunction. Usually, these well-meaning advisors suggest therapy, interventions, and participation in support groups like Al-Anon, ACoA, and CoDA as a way to find support in the process of fully and completely detaching from what they think is a bad situation that's taking the caregiver away from his or her own needs, goals, and personal fulfillment, while keeping the addict mired in the problem.

But what are these assessments based upon?

If you Google codependence, you'll find dozens of lists delineating the core traits of codependent people, several psychological assessments for codependence, and a variety of self-tests for deciding whether you or someone you know is codependent. These resources range from the ACoA's Laundry List to CoDA's Patterns and Characteristics of Codependence to Charles Whitfield's thirty-eight item

Likert-style checklist to the Spann-Fischer Codependency Scale to countless quizzes, lists, and tests provided in blogs, articles, and books on codependence. Regardless of the source, the criteria for codependence inevitably boil down to the following:

- A codependent person makes extreme sacrifices to satisfy the needs of a loved one.
- A codependent person finds it difficult to say no when a loved one makes demands on his or her time and energy.
- A codependent person covers or tries to manage a loved one's problems with alcohol, drugs, money, the law, etc.
- A codependent person sublimates his or her needs to meet the needs of loved ones.
- A codependent person is overly focused (to the point of obsession) on the well-being of his or her troubled loved ones.
- A codependent person has poor boundaries about helping, often doing for addicts (and others) things those people should be doing for themselves.

People who behave in these ways, especially if a loved one is addicted or similarly troubled, tend to be "diagnosed" as codependent. To me, however, these traits sound less like a pathology and more like a person who cares deeply about the well-being of a troubled loved one.

Ask yourself:

- Who doesn't make sacrifices for a person they love, especially if that person is struggling?
- Who doesn't say yes to a family member asking for assistance?

- Who doesn't try to help the family save face in difficult circumstances?
- Who wouldn't sublimate his or her needs to help a struggling loved one?
- Who doesn't worry obsessively when a loved one is struggling?
- Who hasn't overstepped healthy boundaries at least occasionally in a misguided attempt to help a loved one?

WHEN THERAPY DOES MORE HARM THAN GOOD

Michelle is the forty-eight-year-old wife of an active alcoholic. She and her husband, Alex, have three children, ages eleven, fourteen, and twenty-one. For years, Michelle has covered up and attempted to manage Alex's drinking with varying degrees of success. Now her eldest child, Jonathan, is abusing drugs and has dropped out of college. Michelle is perpetually worried that Alex will get fired for missing too much work (he often skips work while binge drinking and recovering from his hangovers) or for showing up at his job while drunk. Meanwhile, Jonathan is living in a crowded two-bedroom apartment with four other dropouts, supporting himself with a part-time, minimum-wage job and a steady stream of "loans" from his parents. For now, the younger children seem to be doing OK in school and socially, but Michelle worries they will follow in their older brother's footsteps or worse.

Unsure about how she should handle everything that she and her loved ones are going through, and terrified about her family's future, Michelle finally seeks therapy and asks for advice for both herself and Alex. After listening to Michelle's gut-wrenching, occasionally teeth-gnashing version of what is happening in her life, her highly recommended therapist offers a bit of emotional support, and then does what she's been taught to do, which is to turn to a disease model for treating loved ones of addicts (codependence) that mirrors the disease model used to treat addicts.

Over the next several weeks, the therapist focuses treatment on Michelle's underlying trauma issues, trying to help her understand that her childhood was less than ideal, and because of this, she learned to relate to others in less than ideal ways, which in turn led her into a codependent relationship with an addict, and that together she and the addict have created less than ideal childhoods for their kids, who are likely to repeat their parents' dysfunctional patterns—as is already occurring with Jonathan—if she doesn't learn to relate to her loved ones differently.

This is frustrating for Michelle, who wants validation for her fears, appreciation for all the giving and caretaking she has done, direction on what to do next, and, most of all, some hope. The seemingly endless talk about her early-life trauma and the damage that has wrought leaves her feeling alienated and shamed. And that does not make sense to her. She is not the addict. She is not the problem.

Because Michelle does not feel heard or understood by her therapist, she often has angry outbursts during her sessions. Unfortunately, as her frustration mounts, her therapist leans more heavily into the codependence model. And why not? After all, the therapist is trained to understand that Michelle's anger and pain are derived from trauma and codependence.

And let's face it, no therapist likes an angry client who screams, yells, cries, blames others, and won't take responsibility. For therapists, it's just plain easier to tolerate all that pain, loss, anger, regret, and fear when we can put a nice, neat label on it, wrap it in a bow, and give it back to the client. So, we turn to codependence as a go-to, even when that model doesn't empathetically meet the client where she is.

Admittedly, some clients do embrace the codependence model and make great strides in a short amount of time. And this makes sense because, even though the framework and conclusions of the codependence model are inherently flawed, the work that loved ones of addicts need to do to heal is nicely laid out in this model. Basically, the codependence model encourages loved ones of addicts to engage in self-care and to set better boundaries with the addict and others in their lives, and this is indeed the work that needs to occur.

What typically does not work is telling loved ones of addicts that their desire to care for the addict is a manifestation of disease. Nevertheless, many caregiving loved ones will (grudgingly) accept the co-dependence label, tacitly agreeing to be pathologized, partly because they are never shown or offered an alternative approach, but mostly because they are willing to do whatever is necessary to help their family heal, even if that means they must sacrifice their own sense of reality.

Unfortunately, plenty of other caregivers will just plain walk away from treatment because they don't feel heard or understood. At worst they feel insulted and judged. At best they feel that what they are being offered does not apply to them. As a result, they and their families don't get the care and guidance they desperately need. That is what happened with Michelle. She stuck it out for a little under two months, felt like she was getting nowhere, and decided to exit therapy. In the end, there was no useful help for Michelle, no useful help for Alex or Jonathan, and no useful help for the younger children. All Michelle got from this experience was a sense of being labeled, blamed, and shamed.

HOW IS THIS HELPFUL?

Sadly, I hear stories like Michelle's far too often. The caregiving loved one of an addict (or multiple addicts) feels hurt, overwhelmed, and fearful, and seeks therapeutic validation and guidance on how to make things better. But instead of receiving warm, empathetic support, the tables are turned. In one way or another, the caregiver is told that he or she is a part of the problem, that he or she has unresolved (possibly unacknowledged) trauma that has led to the disease of codependence, and that he or she is the person who must change.

I ask you, how is this message meeting the client's current emotional needs? In the example above, Michelle is hurt, fearful, and needs validation for what she is feeling. She needs guidance about how she can take better care of herself and how she can love and care for her addicted loved ones and the rest of her family in healthier ways. She needs her therapist to understand that she has exhausted herself trying to "keep it all together" for the sake of her family. She needs her therapist to understand and affirm that she has done this out of love, not because her unresolved early life trauma has driven her into pathological relationships.

When Michelle comes to therapy, that is where she is. And she needs her therapist to be there with her instead of shoehorning her into the blaming and shaming of the codependence model.

In my experience, telling a client like Michelle that she is codependent and needs to detach from a troubled loved one is not sound advice. And I continually hear from other therapists who struggle, as I do, with pinning a pejorative, pathological sounding label on the spouse or parent or sibling of an addict—mostly because these therapists understand that such a client is in crisis and is struggling in the same ways that just about anyone in crisis tends to struggle. So, instead of treating these clients as individuals with a pathology, maybe we should treat them with a model that views them as loving, caring, connection-oriented individuals in crisis. That model is prodependence.

PRODEPENDENCE: A NEW APPROACH

Prodependence is a term I've created to describe attachment relationships that are healthfully interdependent, where one person's strengths support the vulnerabilities of the other and vice versa, with this mutual support occurring automatically and without question. This new model is needed because, as stated above, the codependence model feels negative for many caregiving loved ones of addicts, as if the caregiver is responsible for the addiction because he or she is loving too much, or not in the right way, or for selfish reasons.

Prodependence approaches the matter differently, choosing to celebrate and take healthful advantage of a caregiving loved one's need and willingness to support and stay connected with an addict. With prodependence, there is no shame or blame, no sense of being wrong, no language that pathologizes the caregiving loved one. Instead, there is recognition for effort given, plus hope and useful instruction for healing.

Prodependent Treatment

What if Michelle had encountered a therapist who viewed her issues through a prodependence lens? How would her experience have differed from the one described earlier? And how would she feel about it? Without giving away too much too soon, it might look like a bit like this.

Michelle enters counseling overwhelmed and exhausted from trying to keep her family together. Her husband is broken and unavailable despite her attempts to help him, and her kids are now beginning their own personal journey into dysfunction. All of which leaves her feeling increasingly helpless and somehow at fault.

The professional assigned to help Michelle greets her with open arms, gratefully acknowledging her devotion and sacrifice. "How kind you have been," she tells Michelle, "to have given so much of yourself to those you love. What a gift you are to them." Then, recognizing Michelle's exhaustion and feelings of despair, the therapist says, "You must be so worn out now, and who wouldn't be in your situation? And despite your best efforts things are still slowly but steadily getting worse. I'll bet you're worried that somehow you haven't given enough."

Michelle nods and sobs tears of validation.

After a moment, the therapist says, "You undoubtedly need more support for the good fight you are in to fix your family. After all, how could anyone solve all these problems, no matter how much love they have in their heart? Why don't we work together to see if we can relieve some of your burdens, while at the same time finding the best possible path toward healing your family? Does that sound good?"

- There are no long looks into anyone's past; neither Michelle's nor the family's.
- There is no mention of dysfunction or problems with Michelle or her caregiving (except that she might be overwhelmed and need help).
- There is no criticism of what Michelle has done or challenges to the way she has done it.
- There is no mention of Michelle being "part of the problem."

By leading with prodependence, the professional readily and quickly earns Michelle's trust, helping her feel both understood and supported. And it is from this place of mutual respect and empathy that a path can be made to help Michelle engage in much-needed self-care and set healthy boundaries with her family, all the while working to build an empathetic community of support.

Now, you tell me, in which treatment scenario will Michelle feel more valued, validated, and motivated to work? If you said this one, then you're beginning to understand the power of prodependence.

Before discussing the concept of prodependence in greater detail, I think it's important to examine the thinking and beliefs that led to this new model's formation. This overview begins not with a look at the trauma field, as does codependency, but rather by focusing on attachment—our innate, deeply felt, inherent human need to love, bond with, and care about others. The remainder of the book primarily focuses on prodependence itself—what it looks like, why it's so important, and how to implement the model in treatment. As you read this material, I hope you will do so with an open mind, recognizing that my intent is not to denigrate preexisting approaches or those who created them, but rather to expand that work toward improving the treatment and support we provide to all loved ones of addicts.

Chapter Four

OUR NEED TO CONNECT

Splendid isolation is for planets, not people.[1]

—Sue Johnson, *Love Sense*

HUMANS ARE PACK ANIMALS

Human beings are meant to work together, not to go it alone. For evidence, think back to prehistoric times when people lived in tribes. If we went hunting, we went in a group; otherwise, we were as likely to be eaten as to eat. And hunting trips could take a very long time, so other members of the tribe stayed behind in the cave and tanned hides to keep the group warm, gathered nuts and berries to eat, collected sticks for the fire, and did some rudimentary farming.

For thousands of years, this type of communal living was the standard for survival. Because of this, our brains evolved in ways that encourage interpersonal bonding, and now we are evolutionarily wired to be dependent upon others. We enter the world completely reliant on other people for shelter, nutrition, and emotional support (love), and these core requirements to do not change as we grow older. What keeps us healthy as children also keeps us healthy as adults. Even in late adolescence, when we tend to individuate from our families, we don't move toward isolation. Instead, our dependence needs shift from parents and family to peers and eventually to lovers.

Yet somehow, as we move into adulthood, our intrinsic need for emotional connection gets discounted. This despite the fact that people who spend their lives "apart from" rather than "a part of" do not function as well as those who feel emotionally connected.

An immense amount of mental and physical health research shows that isolated/separated individuals suffer both emotionally and physically.[2] Conversely, people who place a high value on developing and maintaining meaningful connections tend to be happier, more resilient, and more successful.[3] They even tend to live longer.[4] Thus we see that emotionally intimate connections are nearly as essential to life and well-being as more obvious needs like food, water, and shelter.

Without healthy dependency and connection, we may make it physically, but we won't be happy. When we go it alone, we fail to thrive. And this deeply ingrained need for emotional connection does not abate simply because a person with whom we feel an intimate bond is challenged by an addiction or some other serious issue.

As a therapist, I now fully recognize the importance of healthy interdependence throughout our entire life span, and I have come to believe, based on both clinical experience and quite a lot of research, that there is a big difference between enabling or trying to control a loved one's addiction versus continuing to love and care for that person despite his or her life challenges. One set of behaviors (enabling, controlling) is something that clients may need to change, while the other (loving and caring in healthy and productive ways) can be helpful to both the client and the person that he or she cares for.

ATTACHMENT AND EMOTIONAL WELL-BEING

Attachment theory was developed as a psychological construct in the 1940s and '50s by psychologist John Bowlby. In formulating his theories, Bowlby first studied WWII orphans in Europe, finding that even though these children received adequate food, shelter, and physical care, they did not seem to thrive like normal children. Some of them developed so poorly that they died.[5] Based on this observation, Bowlby theorized that the development of emotional bonds might be an evolutionary survival mechanism. Basically, Bowlby felt that wanting *and needing* a constant and reliable source of love and support has evolved into a survival mechanism, every bit as crucial to the existence and success of human beings as opposable thumbs.

In the beginning, Bowlby's theories were almost universally dismissed. (Keep in mind, this was the Dr. Spock era when coddling children was discouraged because it was thought to be counterproductive to their long-term well-being.[6]) Nevertheless, after watching so many war orphans fail to thrive and at times fail to survive, even though nothing appeared to be physically wrong with them, Bowlby kept at it. Eventually, he hired a brilliant Canadian researcher named Mary Ainsworth as his assistant and colleague. It was Ainsworth who devised the breakthrough study, codifying the four behaviors that she and Bowlby saw as essential to healthy attachment:

1) We must monitor and maintain physical closeness with our loved one(s) and caregiver(s).
2) We reach out to our loved one(s) and caregiver(s) when we are upset.
3) We miss our loved one(s) and caregiver(s) when we are apart.
4) We count on our loved one(s) and caregiver(s) to be there for us after we go out into the world to explore and grow.

Ainsworth's now-famed study was called The Strange Situation.[7] In this experiment, Ainsworth and Bowlby put a child and its mother in a room filled with toys and other interesting items, and the mother was instructed to let the child explore the room. After a few minutes, a stranger entered the room and chatted with the mother. Then the stranger turned his or her attention to the child, and the mother left the room. After several minutes, the mother returned to interact with her child, comforting the child if necessary. Then the mother and the stranger both left the room. After a few minutes alone, the mother was sent back into the room to be with her child. During this process, Ainsworth and Bowlby observed the child's reactions to familiar and unfamiliar people, and to being left alone.

Unsurprisingly, the young children were almost always visibly upset when their mother left them with a stranger or completely alone—crying, throwing toys, rocking themselves, etc. Some, however, were less upset than others. They calmed themselves quickly, and they reconnected easily with their mother when she returned. These "emotionally resilient" children seemed confident that their mother would be there when they really wanted and needed her. Meanwhile, the less emotionally resilient children displayed greater degrees of upset when their mother left the room, and greater difficulty reconnecting with her when she returned. They were less confident that she would be there when they needed her.

Notably, Ainsworth and Bowlby noticed that the more easygoing kids had visibly warmer and more emotionally responsive mothers, while the more anxious kids had cooler and less responsive mothers. With this observation, the researchers felt they'd witnessed the power of love in action.

Slowly but steadily, other researchers joined the attachment theory bandwagon. Psychologist Harry Harlow experimented using rhesus monkeys separated from their mothers at birth. He found that the isolated infant monkeys were so hungry for an emotional connection that when they were given a choice between a "mother" made of wire who dispensed food and a soft-cloth mother without food, they invariably chose the squashy rag mother.[8] Harlow also found that these motherless monkeys matured physically but not emotionally. As adults, they failed to understand the social cues of other monkeys, they displayed signs of depression, they were self-destructive, they failed to develop normal problem-solving skills, and they were unable to mate.

We see similar results with humans. Those of us who do not feel securely attached as infants and small children tend to become depressed, anxious, self-destructive, and emotionally isolated as adults. That is a sad fact, but undeniably true. Without a doubt, many people have wonderfully healthy childhoods, and, because of that, they learn to attach securely and healthfully. But many others do not. And I'll bet you can accurately guess which group is more likely to deal with addiction, as either an addict or the loved one of an addict.

THE DEVELOPMENT AND BENEFITS OF "SECURE ATTACHMENT"

In a general way, the best caregivers are responsive to the unique needs of a child, providing the child with emotional regulation, supporting the child's development of self-esteem, and providing a secure base from which the child can comfortably depart, wander, explore, and learn about life—all the while trusting that safety and reassurance can be found when he or she returns to the secure base.

Early in life, a child's forays away from his or her secure base are usually brief. As the child grows, these excursions tend to go further and last longer. Eventually, if managed consistently and with care, the child grows into a separate yet connected and secure adult. Because the child has always had a secure base, he or she is confident with self, others, and the world. In time, the child learns how to provide his or her own internal emotional regulation. This occurs because the securely attached child learns that a healthy response from his or her caregiver(s) is the norm. The child fully believes that support will consistently be there when he or she needs it. The child is secure in this belief and trusts in the goodness and health of the attachment that he or she has developed with family and others.

This is how we learn basic trust in other people.

Unfortunately, when early life caregivers are absent, impaired, addicted, neglectful, anxious, inconsistent, intrusive, mentally ill, overbearing, or similarly unreliable in terms of creating a secure base, a child can orient not to security, but to threat and danger. This experience (more about surviving than thriving) stunts the child's ability to explore the world confidently and to grow in healthy ways. Moreover, the child will tend to feel anxious about self, others, and the world. The child will consistently feel insecure, and as that child grows into adulthood, he or she will likely attempt to cope with that insecurity in one or more of the following maladaptive ways:

- Turning to escapist (often addictive) substances and/or behaviors to avoid feeling emotional discomfort.
- Repeated attempts to bond (to gain a secure attachment) with people who are unable to meet that need.
- Relying on others for self-esteem rather than building self-esteem from within.
- Becoming overly controlling toward others and the environment.
- Becoming overly self-sufficient, walling off the world.
- Failing to trust (failing to become vulnerable and to "let people in"), even when trust is merited and needed.
- Isolating emotionally and/or physically, sometimes in conjunction with an addiction or a psychological disorder (depression, anxiety, etc.).

Once again, as children we require shelter, nutrition, and emotional support, and those needs do not change as we become adults. Admittedly, our need for love and emotional support evolves and looks different as we move from infant to toddler to child to adolescent to young adult to adult. But it does not disappear. And if this need is not met, we suffer. As human beings we have an innate, hard-wired need for emotional closeness, and we ignore this requirement at our peril. To survive and thrive, we need food and shelter, and *we also need love*. Without *all* these necessities, we tend to struggle—as kids, as teens, and as adults.

Secure Versus Insecure Attachment

Over the years, numerous models of attachment have been developed, and they needn't be discussed in detail here. The primary point I want to make is that different people attach in different ways. The short version of the discussion boils down to three basic ideas:

1) We tend to attach either securely or insecurely.
2) Our basic attachment style, be it secure or insecure, develops very early in life—mostly during our infant and toddler years.
3) Our basic attachment style tends to be relatively stable over our life span.

Stated very simply, individuals who experience healthy attachment in childhood, courtesy of responsive caregivers, tend to securely attach as adults. Individuals who do not experience healthy and reliable attachment in childhood tend to struggle with attachment as kids, and also as adults.

The good news is that attachment styles are not set in stone. "Earned security" can be achieved with effort over time, typically through a combination of therapy and the development and nurturance of empathetic, mutually supportive relationships. In this way, people with insecure attachment styles can feel at least relatively secure.

But here's the rub: People who do not have a secure attachment style must learn to attach in healthier ways *by becoming vulnerable* (by risking rejection, abandonment, and everything else that fed into their currently insecure style of attachment). As psychobiologist Stan

Tatkin writes, "If we feel insecure about close relationships, there is no way to become more secure without being in one."[9] So, to overcome our fears about attachment, we must face our fears and become attached. And that is not easy. Especially when the world around us views vulnerability and the dependence we inherently crave as undesirable, overly needy traits.

PERFECT PARENTS ARE CONSISTENTLY IMPERFECT

As discussed earlier, infants and toddlers are hardwired to rely on primary caregivers (usually, though not always, their parents) for safety, comfort, and emotional attunement. Young children naturally and innately seek out the secure base of caregivers in times of emotional and/or physical distress, desiring proximity and security. In the ideal world, a child learns over time to trust others, especially loved ones, because those loved ones are appropriately responsive to the child's needs 100 percent of the time. As a result, the child develops autonomy, feels industrious, cultivates a healthy self-image, believes in himself or herself and his or her abilities, loves, achieves, and feels good about the life that he or she is living.

But is this "perfect" representation of parent-child attachment and bonding really so perfect? No, it is not. If a child's caregivers are responsive 100 percent of the time, the child's development will be stunted, though in different ways than a child who is neglected or abused. When the parent is "perfect," the child never fully experiences or deals with adversity. Consequently, the child never learns to deal with difficulties, never develops autonomy, never feels industrious, etc. Sure, secure attachment may develop, but the individual is nonetheless likely to struggle later in life because he or she has not entirely self-actuated.

This realization has led to the belief that a "good-enough" parent may ultimately be better for a child than a supposedly perfect parent. The good-enough parent is responsive in healthy and appropriate ways enough of the time that the child learns to trust and develops a secure sense of attachment (or at least a *mostly* secure sense of attachment), but the parent is not perfectly responsive all the time. And the parent's imperfection forces the child to grow and to develop in ways that support and encourage self-esteem and self-sufficiency—while still allowing the child to feel (mostly) securely attached.

Interestingly, this same concept holds true in families dealing with addiction. Loved ones of addicts are at their best when they provide relatively consistent and reliable support without being a 100 percent caretaker. So, the best way to care for an addict is to love and support the addict while allowing the addict to grow by living and experiencing his or her life (including addiction-related consequences). There is a happy medium for loved ones of addicts. Enmeshment and control are not good for the addict or the family, but neither is detaching with love and just plain walking away, as the codependency model so often suggests.

SOCIETY VERSUS DEPENDENCE

Sadly, in modern Western culture, being dependent on others is generally viewed as a sign of weakness. In our society, we are taught almost from birth, regardless of gender, that we're on our own, we can't rely on others, and our success and happiness are completely dependent on us and nobody else. We grow up learning that independence, self-sufficiency, and making it through life without the assistance of others is the right way and maybe the only way—even though an immense amount of research tells us the exact opposite is true.

Consider, for instance, a study of married couples where one partner was told that, while in a brain scanner, he or she was going to
receive an electric shock on the ankle every time an X appeared on
a video screen visible in the scanner. When in the scanner alone, the
"danger zones" of these individuals' brains lit up like crazy. The same
was true when a doctor or nurse held their hand to comfort them.
When their spouse held their hand, however, their neurobiological
threat response calmed significantly. Moreover, the level of calming
was directly influenced by the quality of the participant's marriage.
Those with happy marriages were more easily soothed by their partner, and vice versa.[10]

Other studies also support the need for healthy connection. For
example:

- A consistent sense of loneliness can raise blood pressure to the
  point where the risk of heart attack and stroke doubles.[11]
- Distress in an existing relationship increases the risk of heart
  problems.[12]
- Distress in an existing relationship increases the risk of problems with the immune and hormonal systems.[13]
- Social isolation and relationship distress have been linked to
  the common cold.[14]
- Social isolation and relationship distress have been linked to
  lowered odds of surviving a natural disaster.[15]

The research goes on and on, repeatedly revealing an undeniable link between a lack of healthy connections and diminished well-
being. One study suggests that this link is every bit as strong and
every bit as damning as the link between smoking and poor health.[16]

In Personal Terms

About sixteen years ago, a therapist friend said to me, "You know, ever since you moved in with your partner, you seem more focused, more stable, and even more creative." As lovely as that sounds to me today, back then her offhand comment felt more like criticism than validation. In my mind, based on all I'd been taught, I believed that I should be just as successful and together when single as when in a relationship. My upbringing was very clear in this regard: An independent man is stronger and better than one who is dependent and therefore weak. My family and culture taught me from day one that a primary life goal is to be self-sufficient, comfortable with independence, and appreciative of time spent alone. So after my friend essentially told me just the opposite, I wondered *Why is she telling me I seem better off when in a relationship? Does that mean something is wrong with me?*

Looking back on this today—understanding it with the benefit of much hard-won life wisdom—I realize that she was right about me. Moreover, she was explaining one of the basic building blocks of life in a way I had not previously considered. She wasn't speaking in greeting card platitudes like "Life is better when we're together." Nor was she saying that I was a failure or less of a man because I thrived when in a healthy relationship. She simply recognized that I do better with a loving hand by my side. Today, I see my deep need for ongoing connection as a strength. By recognizing, responding to, and anticipating that need today, I feel I am a better person—and a better man.

Research tells us that when we feel securely attached to trusted others, we are healthier, we are more confident, we take more healthy risks, we reach our career goals faster, and we are more willing to explore and take advantage of life opportunities (of all types).[17] So, stated very simply, we do better in all aspects of life when we feel loved and supported. When we feel securely connected, we blossom and grow.

So how can emotional dependence be a weakness?

My friend and colleague, Dr. Sue Johnson, states the matter as succinctly and eloquently as anyone, writing, "Love is not the icing on the cake of life. It is a basic primary need, like oxygen or water."[18] I could not agree more. The Dr. Spock–influenced society of the 1950s got it wrong. We need to hold one another, we need to care for one another in healthy ways, and we need to overtly express our love and have that love returned. Without this, we suffer. Just as we would if we were not eating or sleeping. And this truth does not diminish because we are dealing with a loved one's addiction.

Chapter Five

UNDERSTANDING PRODEPENDENCE

Prodependence: Attachment relationships that are healthfully interdependent, where one person's strengths support the vulnerabilities of the other and vice versa, with this mutual support occurring automatically and without question.

WHAT IS PRODEPENDENCE?

As stated at the close of Chapter 3, prodependence is a term I've created to describe relationships that are healthfully interdependent, where one person's strengths fill in the vulnerabilities of the other and vice versa, with this mutual support occurring automatically and without question. As applied to caregiving loved ones of addicts, prodependence refers to extraordinary, loving attempts to care for and help heal a person to whom one is deeply attached and bonded, even when that person has become chronically dysfunctional because of an addiction or some other equally troubling issue.

Rather than blaming, shaming, and pathologizing loved ones of addicts for loving too much, or not in the right way, or for selfish reasons, or as a form of unconscious trauma repetition, prodependence celebrates their need to love and to caretake when appropriate. Prodependence views the act of loving and trying to help an addict or a similarly troubled individual heal (or to make it through the day without creating or experiencing disaster) as an indicator of healthy attachment (or at least the desire for healthy attachment). With prodependence, there is no shame or blame, no sense of being wrong, no language that pathologizes the client. Instead, there is recognition for effort given, plus hope and useful instruction for healing. To treat loved ones of addicts using prodependence, we need not find that something is "wrong with them." We can simply acknowledge the trauma and inherent dysfunction that occurs when living in close relationship with an addict, and then we can address that in the healthiest, least shaming way.

> To treat loved ones of addicts using prodependence, we need not find that something is "wrong with them." We can simply acknowledge the trauma and inherent dysfunction that occurs when living in close relationship with an addict, and then we can address that in the healthiest, least shaming way.

As with codependence, prodependence recognizes that when a caregiver's actions run off the rails and become counterproductive—and yes, this happens quite a lot when a person is trying to monitor and assist a deeply troubled loved one—measures can be taken to put the relationship back on track. However, prodependence does not imply that a caregiver's dysfunctional behaviors arise out of any past or present trauma or pathology. Instead, prodependence views these actions as an attempt to maintain or restore healthy attachment. Prodependence does not ever consider efforts made to help a loved one get well as pathology, even if those attempts to help are misdirected and ineffective. Under no circumstances does prodependence imply that love is or can become pathological. Instead, prodependence acknowledges that loving an unpredictable, addicted partner who blames, lies, seduces, manipulates, and gaslights loved ones can make pretty much anyone look crazy over time. Because that is the type of behavior that puts people in crisis. And people in crisis can look crazy.

Interestingly, prodependence recommends and implements the same basic therapeutic actions as codependence—a fresh or renewed focus on self-care coupled with implementation of healthier boundaries. That said, the models approach this work from vastly different perspectives. Codependence, as a deficit-based trauma model, views loved ones of addicts as traumatized, damaged, and needing help. Prodependence, as a strength-based, attachment-driven model, views loved ones of addicts as heroes for continuing to love and continuing to remain attached despite the debilitating presence of addiction.

Instead of blaming, shaming, and pathologizing the caregiving loved one of an addict, instead of telling that person that he or she is driven by trauma and needs to deal with that or nothing will change, prodependence says, "You're a wonderful person for putting so much effort into helping your addicted loved one. It's possible, however, that you're not doing that as effectively as you might. And who can blame you for that? It's hard to worry about loving someone in the best possible way when you're in the middle of a disaster zone. If the house is burning down, you grab your loved one and drag that person out of the fire, and you don't worry about whether you're grabbing too hard, or in a way that hurts. Now that you're in therapy, though, we can slow things down and figure out how you can help the addict more effectively—in ways that might be more useful to the addict and your relationship, and that won't cause you to feel so overwhelmed."

Prodependent treatment with caregiving loved ones of addicts recognizes and accepts, first and foremost, that these individuals are, thanks to the addiction, in crisis, and they are likely to behave accordingly. As such, they will show emotional lability. They may also exert superhuman effort with household chores, childcare, doctor's visits, home healthcare, and earning extra money to pay for everything. And they behave in these ways as an expression of love, not pathology.

In short, the prodependence model encourages therapists and clients to celebrate the natural and healthy human need to develop and maintain intimate connections, and to provide ongoing, uninterrupted support to loved ones—even in the face of addiction or some other profoundly troubling life issue.

COMPARING PRODEPENDENCE AND CODEPENDENCE

In many respects, the prodependence and codependence models are mirror images. But with one profound difference. The models vary significantly in how we, as therapists, frame "the problem" to our clients (and ourselves). Consider the following graph delineating traits that are often seen in loved ones of addicts. In the left-hand column, I've listed the negative-sounding words that we see in discussions about codependence. In the right-hand column, I've listed similar traits, but reframed as prodependent positives.

Codependent Versus Prodependent Traits

CODEPENDENT TRAITS	PRODEPENDENT TRAITS
Enmeshed	Deeply involved
Externally focused	Concerned about the welfare of others
Enabling	Supporting
Fearful	Concerned
Lacking healthy boundaries	Eager to care for a loved one
Can't say no	Chooses to say yes
Obsessed with the addiction	Determined to protect the addict and family
Living in denial	Unwilling to give up on a loved one
Angry	Fearful of further loss with no control
Controlling	Trying to be heard
Hypervigilant	Anticipating problems

The expressions of pain and fear that we see with loved ones of addicts are the same with codependence and prodependence. The primary difference lies in *how we frame the problem* to our clients and ourselves. One model is positive and supportive and meets a loving caregiver where he or she is; the other model is the exact opposite, imposing a pseudo-pathology that may cause the client to feel even worse.

Prodependence validates caregiving as the loving act that it is. Prodependence views caregiving loved ones of addicts not as innately damaged, but as relatively healthy people responding to an abnormal situation (addiction in a loved one) as best they can.

Do loved ones of addicts always make the best decisions and go about the business of helping in the best possible way? Of course not. Do they occasionally overstep their bounds in ways that are harmful

> The simple truth is that loved ones of active addicts are perpetually in crisis mode. Naturally, they try to control the crisis. In the process, they sometimes panic and make bad decisions. They may overdo. They may help too much. They may help ineffectively. They may enable and appear to be pathologically enmeshed. But that does not mean they are psychologically disordered.

to themselves and the people they are trying to help? Yes, they do. But why would we expect anything different from a person who is trying to love in a house that's on fire? The simple truth is that loved ones of active addicts are perpetually in crisis mode. Naturally, they try to control the crisis. In the process, they some- times panic and make bad deci-

sions. They may overdo. They may help too much. They may help ineffectively. They may enable and appear to be pathologically enmeshed. But that does not mean they are psychologically disor- dered. What it means is they are *people in crisis*, behaving in the ways that people in crisis tend to behave. And my job as a therapist, when these individuals come to see me, is to meet them where they are, to validate their experience, to value their contributions, and to guide them toward the development and implementation of useful and effective solutions.

Once the crisis stage of healing is past, if a client wants to do deeper forms of inner work (like addressing unresolved trauma), that's great. And that is often what occurs. When the dust has finally settled and the addiction is being adequately addressed, the client will say, "I'm beginning to wonder if anything about the way I grew up might relate to me choosing this person or tolerating the dysfunction of the addiction." At that point, the door is open for deeper work. However, in the early stages of treatment, that's just not where the loved one of an addict is likely to be. And attempting this deeper internal work too soon typically leads a client not to crisis resolution, better boundaries, and improved self-care, but to increased anxiety, self-doubt, and a sense that he or she is part of the problem. This type of shame is counterproductive.

So, once again, loving and caring for an addict is not pathological behavior, even if that love and care occasionally runs off the rails and turns into enabling, enmeshment, and control. Instead, caring deeply and helping fully is a beautiful, wonderful, natural, and life-affirming thing to do. Rather than labeling and pathologizing loved ones of addicts when they refuse to abandon their caregiving roles, I think that my job as a therapist is to thank them for their efforts and encourage them to continue their pursuit of love and emotional intimacy, though in healthier, more prodependent ways.

WHY PRODEPENDENCE?

Family members often struggle to deal with the fact that a loved one is addicted. They also struggle with the fact that in response to their efforts to care for the addict—perhaps taking on extra responsibilities and forgoing personal pleasures and development—the people around them will frequently tell them:

- They have an unhealthy obsession with the addict and his or her behavior.
- They are enmeshed with the addict.
- They are enabling the addiction.

- They are dysfunctionally trying to control the addict's thinking and behavior.
- They are making the problem worse.

Basically, loved ones of addicts are told that their efforts to help are counterproductive and facilitating (maybe even escalating) the problem.

And that might in fact be the case. But even when it is, advising them to "stop rescuing" and to "detach with love" does not account for or even recognize the fact that they can't stop caring for the addict any more than they can stop breathing. What they *can* do is learn to caretake in ways that are more helpful to the addict, and by extension to themselves. They can learn to express love in prodependent rather than obsessive, enmeshed, enabling, controlling, and unproductive ways.

With the prodependence model we can meet spouses, partners, and loved ones of addicts where they are, which is coming from a place of love and a desire for attachment. Rather than telling these folks they are an intrinsic part of the problem, we can acknowledge their hard work and the difficulties they've encountered in trying to help the addict. We can lead them toward caring for themselves as well as the addict, and we can help them provide loving assistance to the addict with better boundaries, all without blaming, shaming, or pathologizing.

In some situations, telling a person that he or she is enmeshed and enabling and needs to detach from a troubled loved one can be downright disastrous. Consider the following true story:

Evan, a forty-eight-year-old single father, learned that his seventeen-year-old son, Oliver, was actively abusing heroin and had been since he was fifteen. From the moment Evan found out about his son's drug use, he blamed himself (and his failed marriage) and, out of love for his son and guilt for his past marital challenges, he did everything he could think of to help. He sent the young man to rehabs, tolerated his stealing from their home to buy drugs, paid his rent after he moved out of the house, and paid for college even though Oliver spent more time getting high than going to class.

When Oliver was twenty, Evan took a good look at how his efforts were paying off, saw no progress, and finally took his therapist's, his CoDA sponsor's, and his friends' and family members' advice to detach with love by walking away. He strongly disagreed with this advice, but his efforts to help had clearly failed, so he surrendered to the idea of letting go and leaving his son to struggle on his own.

Within a year, Oliver was homeless, arrested for theft, and sent to prison for eighteen months. Throughout this ordeal, Evan was continually coached to "detach with love" and to "only give to Oliver when he is sober and doing the right thing." Still, Evan couldn't help but worry about Oliver's safety and well-being.

When Oliver was released from prison, Evan wanted to get him into a drug rehab instead of the depressing halfway house to which he'd been assigned, but again he was advised to "detach with love." And that is what he did. Unfortunately, Oliver was unable to find a decent job, became depressed, started using again, and ended up back on the streets. A week before his twenty-third birthday he overdosed, dying with a needle in his arm just a few miles from his father's home.

When I first saw Evan for therapy a half-dozen or so years ago, his story broke my heart. Without bringing it up to him, I couldn't help but wonder what might have happened if he had been coached toward prodependence rather than detachment. If he had been directed toward maintaining a supportive, well-boundaried relationship with his son—no matter what—perhaps Oliver would have had someone around to catch him before his final fall. Perhaps there would have been a system in place to look out for him—sober or not sober.

It's easy to counsel a parent in a situation like this toward separation from this painful problem, leading with well-worn themes like: "Your son is a man now, and his decisions are his own," or, "You have given him all you can, but now you need to let him sink or swim on his own," or, "You have to let go sometime." While these platitudes may sound like sensible advice on the surface, when an addict goes to prison or dies after a period of detachment, loved ones may have a lifetime wondering if they could have done more, and they may blame themselves for the addict's tragic consequences. Consider this question: Who gets to decide when it's time to give up on someone you love?

With prodependence as his guide, it's entirely possible that Evan would have gotten Oliver into a rehab after prison, and in time Oliver would have found sobriety, a job, and grown into a relatively healthy and well-adjusted person. I've seen such healing occur many times, even under the most unlikely and unexpected of circumstances. You just never know when someone will finally be able to shift his or her life from dysfunction into health. That said, sometimes, it never happens. It's equally possible that this story would have ended the same, with Oliver dead of an overdose. With a prodependent approach, however, Evan wouldn't be blaming himself for *not trying hard enough to help his son*—a regret he will carry for the rest of his days.

In my work today, I don't label or pathologize supporters of challenged individuals who refuse to abandon or diminish their caregiving roles. I encourage them to continue their pursuit of love and emotional intimacy as best they can. At the same time, I provide them with an outline for engaging in self-care and developing and maintaining healthy boundaries—margins within which they can love unconditionally while not enabling, trying to control, doing things their loved one could and should be doing for himself or herself, etc. In so doing, I am revisiting and revising existing ideas related to codependency, caregiving, and caretaking, in the process creating a fresh, nonshaming, attachment-based paradigm for effective and healthy support.

The prodependence model chooses to celebrate a caregiver's desire to love and support an addicted family member when needed. There is no shame or blame, no sense of being wrong, no language that pathologizes the caregiver. Instead, there is recognition for effort given, hope for healing, and useful instruction.

Prodependence recognizes that loved ones of addicts, when first seeking help, are for the most part not ready to look at their deeper personal issues, nor are they able to usefully reflect upon the possibility that these issues might be a contributing factor to the overall problem. What they need and want (and best respond to) in the early stages of healing is empathy for their losses, validation for the loving efforts they have made to help, direction and useful advice about how to more healthfully move forward, and hope about the future.

WHY PRODEPENDENCE IS SO IMPORTANT

As discussed in Chapter 2, addicts use addictive substances and behaviors to self-medicate and self-regulate unwelcome and uncomfortable emotional states. They cope with stress, depression, anxiety, loneliness, boredom, attachment deficits, and unresolved trauma by getting high instead of turning to loved ones and trusted others who might provide emotional support. They use, not to feel *good*, but to feel *less*. And they do this even when their behavior clearly (to an outside observer) creates significant life problems.

Addicts choose addictive substances and behaviors as a coping mechanism over people because, for them, unresolved childhood trauma has poisoned the well of attachment. In the past, people may have hurt them and let them down, leaving them feeling abandoned, unloved, or intruded upon. Thus, they fear emotional intimacy, and they refuse to turn to others—even loved ones—for help when they're struggling. Instead, they self-soothe by numbing out with an addictive substance or behavior.

Over time, to replace the destructive coping mechanisms, addicts must develop healthy ego strength and self-esteem via strong social support—prodependent connections with fellow recovering addicts and loving, empathetic family members and friends. This is the most effective weapon in the sobriety toolbox. It's what sober addicts can turn to when they feel triggered toward relapse.

While this idea may seem obvious to loved ones and therapists, addicts themselves don't necessarily understand it. In fact, active addicts typically engage in their addictive patterns (and related bad behaviors) with little to no comprehension of their motivations. And thanks to this lack of understanding, they may think of themselves as broken and their symptoms as crazy. They simply don't recognize that their upbringing was traumatic and left them without a positive sense of self, and without the ability to fully trust and connect. They don't see and don't understand that their addiction is a maladaptive coping response to their unresolved early life trauma, their negative self-image, and their insecure attachment style.

More important, the only way for addicts to overcome the early life trauma that drives their addiction is to be in relationship with healthy people who treat them with kindness, empathy, and respect. For addicts to overcome addiction, they need to become healthfully attached to people rather than an addictive substance or behavior. Thus, the people around them, especially their loved ones, need to be there for them in healthy, prodependent (nonenmeshed, non-enabling, noncontrolling) ways. This means that caregiving loved ones may need to work on self-care, better boundaries, and other aspects of healthy relationships.

Loving Someone Who Is Mentally Ill

While the emphasis of this book is on loving and caring for an addicted loved one and on addiction in general, the lessons of prodependence are equally applicable and meaningful should a loved one be challenged by mental illness. Loving and caring for a mentally ill individual is no less painful, no less frustrating, and just as all-consuming, as is loving an addict. There is a social stigma associated with mental illness, as well as addiction, and caregivers of both groups often face very similar life challenges.

Throughout the 1980s and well into the early twenty-first century, care-givers of the mentally ill were sadly given the same basic codependence-influenced message as were those involved with addicts: detach with love. Above all—detach. Endless messages repeated the same mantra, most sounding some-thing like this: "Leave them out in the rain if you have to, but don't let them in the house if they're off their meds!" These types of statements were further backed up in support groups. Although this never felt quite right to so many committed spouses, parents, and children, we often did just that. We let them go. For those with chronic emotional illness, often in desperate need of assistance, this single issue has resulted in countless individuals being pushed out in the world on their own, many lacking basic support, some becoming homeless—or worse. As sad and inhumane as it sounds today, professionals back then encouraged family members to turn their mentally ill loved ones away should they be misbehaving, refusing meds or treatment, or otherwise acting out the very symptoms of their illness! Imagine if those with diabetes or heart disease were put out on the street for going off their medications or not following dietary protocols and you can begin to see the problem here.

Happily, over the course of the last decade or so, the mental health sphere has adopted a more solidly prodependent approach. The National Alliance for Mental Illness (NAMI), for instance, today preaches the principles of keeping the family together, advocating for loved ones, not pushing too hard, not giving up, accentuating and celebrating the positive, engaging in self-care, setting healthy boundaries and expecting good behavior while staying aware that crises are inevitable, and staying focused on your larger goals.[1] That is prodependence in a nutshell.

The voice of the mental illness community as a whole has shifted profoundly toward helping families focus on integration and shared support wherever possible rather than distance and separation. Kudos for that change, which can be the difference between life and death. In the world of chronic mental illness, *detachment* can have swift and serious consequences for families and society as a whole. The message promoted by the mental health field today has shifted to one of attachment—keeping families together while teaching them how to lean into one another for strength. Now that's prodependence in action!

Before discussing prodependence in loved ones in detail, I think it's wise to take a slightly more in-depth look at addiction, viewing it as, first and foremost, an intimacy disorder. With that concept in mind, the need for prodependent relating in families affected by addiction becomes even more apparent. This task is undertaken in Chapter 6.

Chapter Six

ADDICTION IS AN INTIMACY DISORDER

You aren't addicted to the substance, you are addicted to the alteration of mood that the substance brings.[1]

—Susan Cheever, *Note Found in a Bottle*

THE ISOLATION OF ADDICTION

Not so long ago, one of the worst possible forms of punishment was not prison or even death; it was exile. For example, in 1814 the controversial military leader, politician, and megalomaniac Napoleon Bonaparte was exiled after ten years as self-proclaimed Emperor of France to the Mediterranean isle of Elba—separated from his wife and son, who were sent to Austria. A year later he escaped, returned to France, and retook his throne for approximately one hundred days before his ultimate defeat at Waterloo. As punishment, they exiled him again, this time to a much smaller and more remote island, St. Helena, 1,000 miles from the nearest land mass in western Africa. Once more, he was sent away without his wife and son. By all accounts, he died a miserable, protracted, and very lonely death on St. Helena.

In the 1800s, you could be drawn and quartered, tortured on the rack, beheaded, hung, and subjected to all sorts of other incredibly nasty punishments. But the meanest, most miserable thing they could think of for Napoleon was exile. And frankly, not much has changed. When people do something wrong in modern society, we send them to prison, a form of exile. And if they misbehave in prison, we put them in solitary confinement, an extra layer of exile.

So, despite the American ethos that constantly tells us we must make it on our own, being alone has long been viewed as a terrible thing. Even American transcendentalists espousing the virtues of solitude seemed to understand this. Consider Henry David Thoreau. Despite what Thoreau's writings might suggest, in the two years he spent at Walden Pond, he was hardly isolated. His cabin, sitting on land owned by his closest friend, Ralph Waldo Emerson, was a thirty-minute walk to the town of Concord, and he traveled there frequently, usually to spend time at the local pub. Thoreau also received frequent visitors at the cabin, most notably his mother, who typically arrived with a home-cooked meal.[2]

Addicts don't seem to get this need for intimacy. They choose to live in emotional exile, and they do not break this exile even if they visit the local pub like Thoreau. In fact, addicts almost universally say they feel most alone when they're in the company of other people. And yes, "other people" includes spouses, family, and other loved ones.

As discussed, this occurs because addicts have learned, usually early in life through neglect, abuse, and other forms of traumatic experience, to fear and avoid emotional vulnerability. Thus, they distance themselves from others, turning instead to addictive substances and behaviors. When addicts become emotionally needful—related to stress, losses, anxiety, depression, and even joyful experiences—they automatically and without conscious thought, turn not to other people but to their addiction, using it as a source of emotional distraction.

Addicts exile themselves in this way because they learned early on that turning to other people for support, validation, and comfort leaves them feeling worse than before they reached out. Thus, they avoid the type of deep relational connections that, for healthier people, bring needed consolation, emotional resolution, stability, consistency, and reward, finding it more familiar and thus easier and emotionally safer to escape and dissociate via substances and behaviors. In short, addicts use their addiction as a maladaptive distraction from their painfully unmet womb-to-tomb emotional dependency needs.

Addictions are not moral failings. Addictions are not weakness. Addictions are not a lack of moral fiber. Addictions are an intimacy disorder.

When addiction is conceptualized in this way—as an intimacy disorder—we can clearly see that the best treatment for addiction is not the pursuit of sobriety; it's the pursuit of healthy, intimate, ongoing connection. Thus, a fundamental task of treatment, once we've gotten addicts through their denial and established a modicum of sobriety, is helping

> When addiction is conceptualized in this way—as an intimacy disorder—we can clearly see that the best treatment for addiction is not the pursuit of sobriety; it's the pursuit of healthy, intimate, ongoing connection.

them develop and maintain healthy and supportive emotional bonds (which, if they remain sober, will serve as the emotional comfort that their addiction never fully provided). It is this approach—not willpower, or babysitters, or shaming, or threatened consequences— that is most likely to lead to lasting sobriety, emotional healing, and a happier, healthier life.

CONNECTION VERSUS ADDICTION

One of the all-time great illustrations of addiction as an intimacy disorder occurs in Canadian researcher Bruce Alexander's famed "Rat Park" study. Prior to Alexander's work, it was generally believed that pleasure, as wrought by addictive substances and behaviors, was the primary driver of addiction. Bolstering this belief was the fact that most early research on the root causes of addiction centered on the neurochemical pleasure response (discussed in Chapter 2), and on the fact that lab rats, when given the choice, would almost always choose to drink opiate-infused water over regular water. For a long while, even the National Institute on Drug Abuse espoused this "plea- sure drives addiction" viewpoint.[3]

However, based solely on the fact that most people do not become addicts (for instance, the Substance Abuse and Mental Health Admin- istration estimates that almost every American adult has tried alco- hol, but only about 6.8 percent become alcoholic[4]), it seemed clear to at least a few addiction treatment specialists and researchers that pleasure was *not* the primary driver of addiction and that the desire for pleasure was *not* what caused some (but not all) people (and rats) to return to a potentially addictive substance or behavior over and over, compulsively and to their detriment.

Recognizing this, Alexander reexamined the results of then-existing rat studies, where test subjects were placed in empty cages, alone, with two water bottles to choose from—one with pure water, the other with opiate-infused water. In those experiments the rats uniformly got hooked on and eventually overdosed on the opiate water, leading researchers to conclude that the out-of-control search for extreme pleasure drives addictions. This led to a belief that addicts were just weak people, and if they could only develop some willpower things would be okay.

Alexander disagreed. He was bothered by the fact that the cages in which lab rats were isolated were small, with no potential for stimulation beyond the opiate water. He thought, "Of course they get high. What else are they supposed to do?" In response, he created the rat park, a cage approximately 200 times larger than the typical isolation cage, with hamster wheels and multicolored balls to play with, plenty of tasty food to eat, and spaces for mating and raising litters.[5] And he put not one rat, but twenty rats (of both genders) into the cage. Then, and only then, did he mirror the old experiments.

And guess what? Alexander's now apparently happy rats ignored the opiate water, expressing much more interest in typical communal rat activities such as playing, fighting, eating, and mating. Even rats who'd previously been isolated and drinking the drugged water left it alone when they were placed in the rat park. With a little bit of social stimulation and connection, addiction in rats disappeared.

My interpretation of Alexander's experiment versus prior experiments is as follows: Putting a rat in a small cage, alone, is a form of exile. That exile mirrors what some traumatized, insecurely attached human beings choose to do to themselves—shutting themselves off from emotional connection and intimacy because they've learned that others, even family members, cannot be trusted. In those circumstances, emotionally and socially isolated humans are exactly like emotionally and socially isolated rats, choosing to use a drug to dull the pain of their exile.

THE HUMAN RAT PARK

One of the reasons rats are routinely used in psychological experiments is that they are social creatures in many of the same ways that humans are social creatures. Happy rats require stimulation, company, play, drama, sex, and social interaction to stay happy.

Humans add an extra layer to this equation. We also need to trust and to securely attach.

As previously discussed, the level and caliber of trust and connection experienced in early childhood carries forward into adulthood, for better or worse. Those who experience secure attachment as infants, toddlers, and children carry that into their adult lives, and they are naturally able to trust and connect in healthy ways. Those who don't experience secure early life attachment tend to struggle with trust and connection as adults. Securely attached individuals tend to feel comfortable in and to enjoy the human version of Alexander's rat park, while insecurely attached people typically struggle to fit in and connect.

And we know by now which group is more vulnerable to addiction, right? We also know from Alexander's work with rats that even rats who'd previously been isolated and drinking the drugged water (addicted rats) left it alone when they were placed in his socially stimulating rat park. With a little bit of socialization, addiction in rats disappeared.

Happily, this result transfers to humans, though in somewhat more complicated ways. With proper direction, support, and a fair amount of conscious effort, individuals who were not graced with secure childhood attachments (and therefore the ability to easily and comfortably connect in adulthood) can develop earned security via long-term therapy, faith-based and twelve-step groups, and various other healthy and healing relationships—the most important of which are healthy connections with loved ones.

> With proper direction, support, and a fair amount of conscious effort, individuals who were not graced with secure childhood attachments (and therefore the ability to easily and comfortably connect in adulthood) can develop earned security via long-term therapy, faith-based and twelve-step groups, and various other healthy and healing relationships—the most important of which are healthy connections with loved ones.

This means the dysfunctional lessons learned by addicts in childhood can be unlearned (experienced differently) through empathetic and supportive emotional interactions, especially with loving, empathetic, healthfully supportive family members and friends. Addicts are not automatically locked for life into a state of isolated self-soothing and self-regulation.

However, placing human addicts in a room full of people and stimulating activities (as Alexander did with rats) is not quite enough. Human addicts must earn a sense of security and attachment. Rats don't really need to do that because their brains and their psyches are considerably simpler. You can take an addicted rat and toss him into the rat park, and he will quickly and easily assimilate, pushing his addiction to the curb in favor of healthier rat connections and activities.

People? Not so much. With human addicts, there is further work to be done.

Interestingly, addiction treatment specialists and the twelve-step community have unconsciously operated with "addictions are an intimacy disorder, and healthy connections are the antidote" as an underlying principle for decades. In fact, much of what occurs in well-informed, group-focused addiction treatment programs and twelve-step recovery programs (beyond breaking through the addict's denial and putting a stop to the addictive behavior) is geared, either directly or indirectly, toward the development of reliably healthy social bonds.

Admittedly, twelve-step programs are not the right path for every recovering addict. However, those who have found sobriety and peace in places like AA, NA, SAA, and CMA almost universally find in those environments a safe place to explore, practice, and develop relationships and social bonding. And trust me here, addicts don't attend twelve-step meetings for years on end for the coffee and doughnuts. They stick around because the rooms of recovery are where they finally feel like they're part of a healthy, responsive, supportive, and engaged family.

Interestingly, it's not just therapists, support groups, and loved ones who can help addicts. Society at large can also lend a hand. Consider the nation of Portugal. Since decriminalizing illicit drugs in 2001, Portugal has tried very hard to integrate addicts into their communities, offering traditional treatment and counseling plus subsidized jobs and quite a lot of social programming. Basically, Portugal has made a nationwide effort to help addicts *connect* with the world and the people around them. And it's working, too. Problematic drug use is down, including adolescent drug use, drug-related harms, and drug-related deaths.[6] Portugal's strategy of connecting instead of incarcerating (exiling, isolating, and disconnecting) addicts has been highly effective.

And why would we expect anything different? After all, as we have discussed, it's an essential part of the human condition to attach emotionally and to lean into our attachments. This need for connection is as fundamental to life, health, and happiness as our needs for food, water, and shelter. When our needs for intimacy and attachment go unmet, we struggle. End of story.

That said, developing healthy intimate connections can be difficult, especially for addicts, who, as discussed, nearly always have histories of chronic childhood trauma and other forms of early life dysfunction that make intimate attachment uncomfortable and difficult. For addicts, learning to trust, reducing shame, and feeling comfortable with both emotional and social vulnerability takes time, ongoing effort, and a knowledgeable, willing, and empathetic support network (therapists, fellow recovering addicts, friends, employers, and, of course, prodependent loved ones). The good news is that both research and countless thousands of healthy, happy, long-sober addicts have shown us that such healing can turn an isolated and addicted life into a life of joy and connection.

BASIC ADDICTION TREATMENT

With addicts, we use a wide variety of treatment methodologies —behavior based, trauma based, attachment based, etc. Whatever modality is used, addicts nearly always need, first and foremost, a giant dose of reality. Beyond initial sobriety and ensuring they are stable enough to begin treatment, breaking through the façade of denial that allows them to use with (internal) impunity is task number one. Little forward movement can occur until they understand and view their addiction as the destructive force that it is.

Once denial cracks, which can be a difficult and time-consuming process, a plan for ongoing sobriety (that incorporates lots and lots of truth-telling, trust-building, and accountability) can be implemented. Usually, this plan incorporates a mix of individual therapy, addiction-focused group therapy, cognitive behavioral work, social learning, and twelve-step or similar support groups. Ultimately, addiction treatment recognizes that the disease of addiction is, more than anything else, an intimacy disorder, and these various approaches tend to work mostly because they encourage healthy human interactions and connection.

At some point, addicts are also asked to identify and eventually to address the underlying emotional deficits and trauma that lead them into addiction in the first place. At minimum, reviewing a client's trauma history helps to reduce shame. Essentially, this effort tells addicts, "You're not an addict because you're a bad person. You're an addict because some bad things happened when you were younger, and you cleverly learned to escape your painful emotions by numbing out. Unfortunately, you're still handling your problems by escaping from them instead of turning to others for help in dealing with them."

Whichever approaches are utilized in treatment, the work required for early addiction healing looks something like this:

- Identify the addictive patterns.
- Stop the drinking/using/acting out.
- Engage in immediate crisis management.
- Break through the addict's denial about the nature and consequences of addictive behavior.
- Identify addiction triggers (the people, places, and things that precipitate a need/desire to use).

- Identify and implement alternatives to using (healthier ways to cope with triggers).
- Examine past trauma—abuse, neglect, and other issues that have created an inability to trust and securely attach, and therefore a tendency to escape emotional discomfort by numbing out rather than turning to other people for support.
- Develop earned security through prodependent connections with clinicians, fellow recovering addicts, friends, and most importantly, loved ones.

So, once again, treating addicts ultimately focuses on the development of prodependent connections with loved ones and other important individuals. Simply stated, addiction treatment encourages and facilitates a transition from addiction dependency to interpersonal dependency. This is why it's important for caregiving loved ones to learn prodependent ways of relating. When loved ones of addicts are healthfully prodependent, it's easier for addicts to feel safely connected. And when addicts feel safely connected, it's easier to stay sober.

Chapter Seven

APPLIED PRODEPENDENCE

If a problem can't be solved within the frame it was conceived,
the solution lies in reframing the problem.[1]

—Brian McGreevy, *Hemlock Grove*

A LOVED ONE'S ROLE IN THE
HEALING PROCESS

As stated earlier, addicts learn early in life from thousands of small interactions plus a couple of highly formative events that relying on others for emotional support is confusing and chaotic and best avoided. The thought of attaching to the degree and in the ways that healthier people tend to attach creates anxiety and fear. As such, addicts are unlikely to ask for support no matter how badly they need it, and, just as importantly, they are unlikely to willingly receive support when it's offered.

This is where caregiving loved ones come in. As discussed in Chapter 6, the most effective way to overcome addiction is for addicts to develop healthy, meaningful, ongoing interpersonal connections. Unquestionably, the most important of those connections are with prodependent loved ones. Ideally, these individuals are an integral and ongoing part of an addict's recovery because slowly and steadily developing a secure base—developing earned security with loved ones—helps an addict heal from addiction long-term.

When an addict finally learns that he or she can trust loved ones to be there in healthy and supportive ways, the addict has a secure base that he or she can turn to in the chaos. And that makes staying sober much easier. It also makes uncovering, processing, and healing from the early life traumas that underlie the addiction (because they've poisoned the well of attachment) considerably easier, though that process can still be incredibly difficult.

The fear, of course, is that caregiving loved ones might (and occasionally do), as a way of keeping the relationship intact, behave in ways that enable and perpetuate the addiction. Still, the solution is not detachment, where caregivers love the addict but only from afar. The solution is to stay connected and to continue caregiving, but to do that more effectively.

Unfortunately, this is not what our culture (either clinical or popular) currently teaches. Addicts are told to pull themselves up by their bootstraps, and caregivers of addicts are advised to detach with love. This advice helps neither the addict nor the addict's loved ones because the healthiest way of dealing with problems is *with* empathetic others. Facing the dragon alone just doesn't work very well. And let's remember, addicts turn to addictive substances and behaviors because they've been taught that others either cannot or will not support them in healthy ways. A loved one detaching from them when they need that person the most does nothing to counter this self-destructive, addiction-driving belief.

In my opinion, caregiving loved ones should be coached to continue caregiving, to continue fighting to stay attached. Because with addicts, healthy attachment is a key facet of recovery. That said, the type and quality of attachment and support that loved ones provide matters. A lot. Enabling behaviors, disguised as helping behaviors, will keep the addict (and the family) stuck in the cycle of addiction. Meanwhile, attempts to control the addiction and its consequences will push the addict into an emotional bomb shelter—where he or she can weather the drama-filled onslaught of the caregiver's misdirected love without ever addressing the addiction.

Do you remember the Karpman Drama Triangle discussed in Chapter 3? In this dynamic, caregivers and addicts bounce cyclically from one corner of the triangle to another in a dysfunctional *pas de deux*. They dance from the persecutor corner to the rescuer corner to the victim corner, each person taking a role and pushing the other person's buttons until they both get sick of it and move to different corners, where there are different but equally destructive buttons to push.

With prodependence, the goal is not to move the loved one and the addict from one dysfunctional corner of a triangle to another, it's to guide them from dysfunctional relating to healthier relating. This, of course, does not happen overnight. The goal is to move both loved ones and addicts incrementally across the relational continuum, one step at a time, toward prodependence and healthier relating. In time, this can facilitate the healthy, secure bonding that pulls addicts into the healthy human's version of the proverbial rat park.

That said, caregivers need to consistently be safe people for this to occur, and in the early stages of a family's healing, it's likely that they're not—usually because they lack the necessary boundaries. As such, loved ones often need to take a step back in early recovery, letting the addict rely more on his or her therapist, therapy group, and twelve-step fellowship than on family members. At the same time, loved ones can work to improve the ways in which they relate to, connect with, and care for the addict. To this end, they must learn to care for themselves as well as the addict, and to set and maintain better boundaries.

If you're familiar with codependence work, the preceding paragraph likely sounds familiar. And it should because *this is the exact same stepping away and engaging in self-care and boundary work that codependence recommends.* However, as stated earlier, prodependence recommends this work from a different perspective. Codependence tells loved ones they're traumatized and damaged and driving the dysfunction in their family, and, until they step away and make changes, the situation will either stay the same or get worse. Prodependence tells loved ones they're doing hero's work, but there are ways they can do that more effectively while also taking better care of themselves.

In the caregiver's mind, that is a huge difference.

LOVED ONES OF ADDICTS IN THERAPY

With prodependence, caregiving loved ones of addicts are not automatically "diagnosed" as having an illness requiring treatment. Instead of viewing caregivers as part of the disease, prodependence views them as being in crisis and behaving as anyone in crisis would naturally behave. Caregivers are not thought of as struggling because of an inherent pathology (or even a pseudo-pathology), they are thought of as struggling because:

> Instead of viewing caregivers as part of the disease, prodependence views them as being in crisis and behaving as anyone in crisis would naturally behave.

- A person with whom they are deeply bonded is failing, despite all attempts to assist and care for that person.
- They find themselves inadvertently behaving in ways that cause them to feel badly about themselves, like nagging, yelling, threatening, enabling, judging, etc.
- They are confused, exhausted, and overwhelmed (in crisis) because they've been doing their job and the addict's job within the family at the same time, often for years on end.
- They feel defeated, unloved, unappreciated, and hopeless due to the addict's inability to stop using (despite their best efforts to help).

Recognizing this, prodependent treatment for loved ones of addicts goes as follows:

- Assess for any genuine pathology (depression, anxiety, PTSD, mood disorders, and the like).
- Validate and celebrate prior attempts to rescue, save, heal, and otherwise help the addict.
- Educate about the nature of addiction and the stress it can place on loved ones.

- Identify times and situations where a loved one's actions have led to a less than ideal outcome, and redirect toward more effective assistance.
- Work to establish, implement, and maintain healthy boundaries with the addict and others.
- Work to improve the client's efforts at self-care—exercise, recreation, spirituality, creativity, etc.
- If, over time, the client seeks deeper understanding of his or her trauma history, that door can be opened, but only after the crisis stage has passed and the client's life is stabilized.

Addictions are difficult and confusing disorders for anyone to tolerate in someone they love. Always. It's not just the pain of specific bad behaviors on the part of the addict that they must overcome, it's their *loss of trust* in that loved one. Addicts lie, cheat, mislead, keep secrets, and gaslight the people who love them. This loss of trust leaves caregiving loved ones in a daze—stunned, hurt, uncertain, and unable to fully assimilate and accept what has happened. Recognizing this, therapists should avoid attempts to:

- Look at the client's role in the addiction and the family's problems.
- Explore the client's childhood and family history.
- Diagnose the client (as codependent, bipolar, borderline, or anything else) as a way of explaining the client's distress.

In the early, crisis stage of treatment, these efforts are not helpful. What caregiving loved ones of addicts do need is:

- Validation of their intuition and feelings.

- Acknowledgment and appreciation for the love and care they have provided.
- Structure for day-to-day life, geared toward simple survival and moving forward.
- Education about addiction and the family dynamics of recovery.
- Insight into the effects that lies, manipulation, and secrets have on loved ones of addicts.
- Concrete direction regarding in-the-moment and longer-term self-care.
- Useful advice on setting and maintaining healthy boundaries with the addict and others.
- Hope

Loved ones of addicts also need therapists and others to understand, accept, and validate that they have every right to feel angry, hurt, confused, and mistrustful. Thus, they may understandably rage, split, decompensate, do detective work, enmesh, enable, control, try to get an opinion from anyone they can find, and more. This is their perfectly normal reaction to the crises wrought by their loved one's addiction.

Instead of being confrontational or overtly directive with people who love and care for addicts, we need to be invitational. We need to meet them where they are, focusing less on detachment and more on supporting their addicted loved one in healthier, more prodependent ways. Rather than preaching detachment and distance over continued bonding and assistance, as so many therapists, self-help books, and twelve-step groups currently do, we should celebrate the human need for and pursuit of intimate connection, using that as a positive force for change.

LOVED ONES CAN BE THE LAST
(YET MOST IMPORTANT) CONNECTION

For reasons already discussed, intimate connections are difficult for addicts, including addicts who are early in the recovery process. Because of this, addicts new to sobriety often find it easier to connect and be supported through external sources like therapy, church groups, twelve-step recovery, and other addiction-focused support networks. These "less important" connections are less threatening to newly recovering addicts. This can be confusing and traumatic for family members, who feel shunned when the addict opts to connect with and rely on others but not them.

A caregiving loved one's job during this trying period is to be there in healthy, prodependent ways when the addict is ready and willing to accept the loved one's support, even if that means the loved one is the last person invited to the recovery party. Caregivers need to understand that when the addict pushes them away, it's not because the addict doesn't love and care about them, and it's not because the addict doesn't want to be cared for and loved by them; it's because the addict feels unworthy of love and support, especially from the people who "know them" the best. This is why we can drop a human addict into a healthy social situation—the human version of the rat park— and he or she is unlikely to recover without further effort. Humans with attachment issues don't overcome those problems simply by being around other people. They need to *safely connect* on an emotionally intimate level. They need to develop *earned security*. And for addicts that is easier accomplished, at least initially, with relative strangers than family members.

That said, it's pretty awful for caregiving loved ones when an addict is willing to become emotionally connected with and to accept support from a therapist, a priest, a sponsor, friends, and fellow recovering addicts and not them. But starting with those far away and slowly working back to intimately attach with those who are closer and more important is often an addict's pathway to connection.

Addicts take baby steps in recovery, learning to become vulnerable (and to accept the rewards of doing this) a little at a time. The less important a relationship is to the addict, the easier it is to take a risk and move forward in that relationship. When viewed in this way, being the last person that the addict becomes vulnerable (and truly intimate) with can be thought of as a compliment—because this is the relationship the addict is most afraid of losing. It is essential that therapists help loved ones of addicts understand this.

WHO CAN LOVED ONES TURN TO FOR SUPPORT?

In the midst of crisis, the natural thing for a person to do is to turn to a loved one for support. That person loves you, and you love that person, so you are going to be there to support each other. And the closer you are to that person, the more likely it is that he or she will be able and willing to care for you. Unless, of course, that loved one is an addict. Because addicts just don't connect in this way.

My colleague Michelle Mays refers to this conundrum—the desire to turn to a loved one for support even though that person, because of an addiction, is ill-equipped to respond in healthy, empathetic, supportive ways—as the no man's land of recovery.[2] Usually, loved ones of addicts are all too familiar with this space. They innately know that they need to connect with a loved one to heal the attachment deficit they feel, but their loved one, because he or she is addicted, can't provide the needed support and connection.

Even when the addict is doing everything possible to establish and maintain sobriety, the pain that he or she has caused to caregiving loved ones is usually too deep and too fresh for the addict to be trusted and relied upon in any meaningful emotional way. As such, the addict is poorly suited to providing support even if he or she were psychologically willing to do so, which, for reasons already discussed, is unlikely in early recovery. This realization can be painful for both parties. They know that they love and care for one another, but the addiction has driven a wedge between them that makes healthy intimacy difficult.

In time, this will change. In the early stages of healing, however, loved ones of addicts, like addicts themselves, typically need to look elsewhere for support—to prodependence-oriented therapists, to friends who can empathize with and validate their experience, and to support groups that can help them focus, at least a little bit, on caring for themselves as well as their addicted loved one. And yes, this type of support can be found in groups like ACoA and Al-Anon—as long as the individual focuses on the work at hand (boundaries, self-care, attending to themselves as well as their troubled loved one) while not buying into the belief that their love, support, and caregiving are inherently unhealthy.

And yes, I fully understand that I have spent this entire book arguing that we need to move beyond the codependence model of the past, and it may seem antithetical for me to now suggest that loved ones of addicts can benefit from groups like ACoA and Al-Anon. But plenty of people do find meaningful social support, useful advice, and much-needed connection in these groups. And this can occur even when they don't buy into "the need for detachment from the addict" because the rest of the work in these fellowships tends to focus on improved self-care and better boundaries—tasks inherent to healing.

SELF-CARE

As stated above, when working with loved ones of addicts, there are two primary areas of focus: self-care and healthy boundaries. Often, convincing loved ones to concentrate, even a little bit, on their own well-being is the more difficult task.

When dealing with caregiving loved ones who are reluctant to also care for themselves, I sometimes remind them that on airplanes flight attendants instruct passengers on safety procedures in the event of an emergency. One of their primary instructions is that, if oxygen masks are needed, parents should affix their mask first, and then affix masks on their children. This directive recognizes a fundamental tenet of life: If you're not taking adequate care of yourself, you're likely to be a poor caregiver for others. This is especially true on oxygen-depleted airplanes and when dealing with an addict.

Nevertheless, self-care often sounds selfish to caregiving loved ones, even though it's not. Unless, of course, the person flips to the opposite extreme and completely stops caring for others. Detaching to that degree is as unhealthy as focusing on others to the point where one forgets to care for oneself. Self-care does not mean caring for oneself *instead of* the addict, it means caring for oneself *as well as* the addict.

With prodependence, self-care is about finding a middle ground that is healthy for the caregiver, for the addict, and for the relationship between the caregiver and the addict. Living in the

> With prodependence, self-care is about finding a middle ground that is healthy for the caregiver, for the addict, and for the relationship between the caregiver and the addict.

extremes—doing too much too often or detaching completely and forcing the addict to struggle without assistance—is not healthy for anyone. Living in one or the other of these extremes perpetuates the addiction, along with insecure attachment, family dysfunction, and an unhappy life.

Still, engaging in self-care may feel counterintuitive to caregiving loved ones who are so used to focusing on someone else. Often, they learned in childhood that their needs were not important and the only way for them to get attention was to subjugate themselves and focus on the needs, wants, and desires of others. In such cases, taking time out to care for oneself seems decadent. For individuals who are used to being ignored, deprived, shamed, and used, as loved ones of addicts often are, pausing to engage in even a small of amount of self-care and self-nurturance typically requires external guidance, support, a great deal of conscious planning, and structured accountability.

To My Fellow Professionals:
Codependence à la Carte Is Still . . . Codependence

While writing this book, I spoke to many of you about your current use of the term and model of codependency. My thanks to you for offering your time, beliefs, experiences, interpretations, and opinions. What I have heard almost universally is that we have a shared need for a fully articulated, differently focused model for the treatment of addict's loved ones—a model that goes beyond the constraints of codependency as it is generally viewed and practiced.

It appears to me, after these conversations, that many of you are on this new pathway already, though without terminology or a guidebook to light the way. In our discussions many of you have said things to me like:

- I use an adapted version of the codependency model, but mine is more attachment focused.

- I see codependence as a developmental issue, as laid out in some of the later writings on the subject, and not as much about early-life trauma, as many others tend to view it.
- I use the word *codependent,* but I don't use that actual model for treatment because my clients typically don't respond well to it.
- I work from adaptive, later versions of the codependence model, ones written long after the original model was proposed. And even then, I focus more on healthy attachment than detachment.
- I don't do much, if any, trauma exploration at the start when I'm treating loved ones of addicts. I use more of a crisis-driven model.

To you I say, "Great job! You have already found (or are finding) your way to prodependent, attachment-focused treatment for caregiving loved ones of addicts and other troubled individuals, and you were doing this before I ever put pen to paper. I celebrate your useful additions and adaptations to this new model of prodependence. Moreover, your thoughtful input has helped me evolve my own theories and the text of this book."

That said, I cannot rely on the codependence model, even an adapted version, as so many of the people I've spoken with have chosen to do. Codependence will always be a trauma-based model that looks to the past to see how/why/where past trauma is affecting a loved one's present. That is the model, plain and simple, as written.

To move beyond codependency, we must acknowledge that no matter how evolved or adaptive, no matter how progressive, integrative, deeply supportive, useful, and non-pathologizing your work may be, it is time to stop referring to it as codependence work. If you are not working within the codependence model as organized and written by those who very clearly laid out their beliefs and intentions nearly forty years ago, then you are doing something else. For those who want to work within other forms of partner treatment, ones that significantly differ from the codependence model as it was originally laid out and as it is generally interpreted, I'm with you. But we must refer to this work as something new, and something other than codependence. Working with the loved ones of addicts and other troubled people doesn't mean you are working with someone who is "codependent."

BOUNDARIES

Many addicts try to get healthy and succeed. They get sober, they stay sober, and they slowly overcome the trauma and other issues that have kept them "apart from" instead of "a part of." Other addicts repeatedly try and fail to get sober. Sometimes they have no real interest in sobriety, even if they pretend otherwise. And these outcomes have very little, if anything at all, to do with the loved ones who care for them. An addict's sobriety is not dependent on his or her loved ones. Recovery is the purview of the addict and no one else.

Still, loved ones of addicts feel responsible for the safety, well-being, and recovery of the addict. Because of this, they often find themselves doing one or more of the following:

- Taking care of things that are the addict's responsibility, not theirs.
- Doing things they don't want to do because they feel like they have no choice.
- Meeting (what they perceive to be) the addict's needs without the addict asking for help.

- Forcing their assistance on the addict, even when that assistance is not wanted or needed.
- Giving and giving and giving but never receiving.
- Focusing more on the problems of the addict than on their own problems.
- Focusing more on the feelings of the addict than on their own feelings.
- Making excuses for and/or covering up the problematic behavior of the addict.
- Becoming indispensable to the addict as a way of keeping the addict close.
- Trying to control the addict's behavior as a way of keeping the addict safe.

Consider the words of Hayley, the thirty-two-year-old wife of an alcoholic:

> I was sure that if I could just do a better job with the house and kids, cook better meals, be better in bed, and convince him of my love for him, he would stop drinking. I honestly thought that if I could just be the perfect wife, he would sober up and everything would be OK, and we would finally be happy. What I didn't understand was that drinking was his problem to fix, not mine.
>
> If you can think of it, I probably tried it. But nothing I did worked. He just kept on drinking, and his life—our life—continued to fall apart. I found myself trying to manage and control one crisis after another while micromanaging every aspect of his life. I continued to do this even when I knew it was making me miserable. I just couldn't stop. I was too afraid of the consequences. I worried that if I didn't stop him from drinking, he might get another drunk driving ticket and go to jail for many months, or

he might drink and drive and kill someone and go to jail for many years, or he might drink and drive and kill himself. Then there was the fear that if I pushed him too hard to get sober, he would get angry and leave me. Still, I couldn't stop yelling and screaming and manipulating and fixing and doing all sorts of other things to control the addiction. Eventually, I was so busy trying to manage his life that I wasn't living my own.

Hayley's desire to bond with and care for her husband, coupled with her anxiety about being alone and unloved, caused her to try to control aspects of her husband's life that were not hers to control. She meant well, but she tried to do too much. Her lack of boundaries and attempts to manage her husband and his alcoholism were a far cry from the healthy, prodependent interaction that he (and she) needed. In time, her "protection" became a prison in which she and her husband were confined.

Hayley, rather obviously, needed help with healthier boundaries. However, like many loved ones of addicts, she didn't understand that many of her efforts to care for her husband were, in fact, counterproductive. She did not understand that by nagging, enabling, and trying to control, she took away her husband's sense of responsibility, along with his ability to make decisions and solve problems, learn from his mistakes, grow as a person, and achieve sobriety, recovery, and healing.

In therapy, rather than point this out to Hayley, perhaps diagnosing her as a classic codependent, I complimented her on her fortitude and for sticking with her husband even in the face of addiction. Then we talked about how tiring and emotionally draining this was for her. Eventually, I suggested that there might be some better, more effective, and less draining ways for her to care for her husband, letting her know that would likely involve setting some boundaries.

To this, Hayley responded as many loved ones of addicts do, saying, "I've done that. I've set boundaries, and he's broken them. Over and over. It doesn't work. He won't change his behavior just because I set a boundary."

I smiled at Hayley's response. Loved ones of addicts often seem to think that setting boundaries is about putting limits on the *addict's* behavior. And inevitably they've learned, as does anyone who has tried to control the behavior of another person (who's over the age of twelve), that this does not work—at all. Because other people don't want to be controlled by us any more than we want to be controlled by them.

This means that caregivers must focus on their own behavior, not the addict's when reviewing relationship boundaries. I explained this boundary basic to Hayley using my two favorite analogies for boundaries. The first analogy is that healthy boundaries are about staying in our own hula hoop, meaning the only things we can control or that we should try to control are the items within our immediate space—the things that fit within our hula hoop. The second analogy is that we must sometimes look at a situation that's out of control and say, "Not my circus, not my monkeys." If a problem is not of our making, then it's probably not ours to control or fix, and we should leave it alone.

I also explained to Hayley that the purpose of healthy boundaries is to facilitate healthy relationships, not to shut relationships down. Healthy boundaries are not about keeping other people out; they're about letting other people safely in. If other people are behaving in ways that are safe for us, we can choose to let them in. If they are behaving in ways that are not safe for us, we can choose to keep them out.

> Healthy boundaries are not about keeping other people out; they're about letting other people safely in.

Their behavior belongs to them; our choice belongs to us.

Finally, I let Hayley know that when properly implemented, healthy boundaries prevent enabling, enmeshment, and unwarranted attempts at control. In this way, boundaries protect caregivers from bad behavior by the addict, and, just as importantly, they protect the addict from bad behavior by the caregiver. In time, with healthy boundaries, a caregiver and an addict can establish and maintain healthy inter-dependence in their relationship.

That said, boundaries are not a one-size-fits-all proposition. Boundaries that are helpful in some relationships could be very unhelpful in others. Recognizing this, I generally ask loved ones of addicts, such as Hayley, to answer the following questions before attempting to define and implement healthy boundaries:

- How deeply mired in addiction is your loved one? Does the addiction completely control the addict's life and thought process, or can the addict still (at least occasionally) make intelligent, rational, well-reasoned decisions?
- Would pulling back and letting the addict face the consequences of the addiction be helpful in terms of motivating his or her recovery?
- What would those consequences likely be? Are those consequences something that you and the rest of the family can live with?
- What aspect of the addiction frightens you most? What aspect of the addiction do you most want (and try) to control? Is this a fear that you can rationally and legitimately release?
- Is this a situation where the best thing would be to do more and not less? Despite everyone's desire to see the addict assume responsibility for himself or herself, could this be a situation

where more of you (as a caregiver) is needed? Could it be time to hold steady on the reins and not let go?

Healthy boundaries need to be set on a case-by-case basis. What works for one relationship might not work for another. Moreover, the creation of healthy boundaries can mean pulling back on control, as with Hailey and her husband, or taking more control, as we will see in the example that closes this chapter. And sometimes the difference between the two situations is not entirely clear. That is the difficulty faced by loved ones of addicts. As such, the process of finding what works and what doesn't is a matter of trial and error. Moreover, what works and what doesn't work may change over time as the addict starts to heal and become more accountable. As a prodependence-oriented therapist, my job is to facilitate the process of setting and maintaining healthy boundaries (in either direction) while encouraging motivation, structured change, and hope.

No matter how frustrated I may at times get with a client's seeming inability to implement healthy boundaries, I need to remember that telling the caregiving loved one of an addict to "just stop enabling and controlling" is about as useful as telling an addict to "just stop using." So, not at all. A better, more prodependent approach is to help the caregiver build healthy interdependence and connection with the addict over time by establishing boundaries that are realistic and workable for that person in that relationship at that time. No more, no less.

WHEN LOVE MEANS MORE, NOT LESS

If you're wondering about a situation where more rather than less control is the healthiest boundary to set, consider the case of Jamie.

As a nineteen-year-old freshman, Jamie was not doing well in his first year at college. Despite a solid high school record, reports from the academic advisory office to his parents showed that he was barely passing three of his classes, and if his grades did not improve, he was likely to go on academic probation.

This news was surprising and disturbing to Jamie's folks, who had always known their son to be a consistent and steady achiever. Their first instinct was to go to the school and check on him, but, assured by the college that early struggles are not unexpected for new students, they backed off this plan. They decided they shouldn't get too involved too soon. Plus, they wanted their son to "have his college experience." Although they were worried and their inaction didn't quite feel right to them, they left the situation alone. However, a call came barely a week later, informing them that their son had been in a car wreck and they needed to get to the hospital right away.

Apparently, Jamie had been out binge drinking with some other students—including the driver, who'd passed out at the wheel. When his parents arrived, Jamie was awake and only mildly injured, with a few broken fingers and some painfully bruised ribs. After a lot of hugs and tears, the family conversation began in earnest. Jamie's parents were determined; he was not ready to be off on his own. Citing his poor academic performance and the danger of the situation he had just been in, they told him that their minds were made up. Jamie needed—and was going to get—a slower start. This meant going back home and attending community college for at least a year.

Jamie did not take the news well, viewing his parents' move as punishment and a way to keep him away from his new friends. Despite his tearful protest and pleas for them to reconsider, his parents held firm. They knew their son, and he wasn't ready. So Jamie got dragged back home kicking and screaming that very night.

Much to Jamie's surprise, within a few weeks he found that he liked being back at home. Without the social pressures and the strain of learning to live on his own, he was able to focus on his classes. And when he was certain he could handle the academic workload, he took on a part-time job to help with expenses. He also rekindled an old romance. Instead of bad grades, drinking binges, and general instability, Jamie was suddenly doing well and growing.

This is prodependent love and healthy boundaries in action.

Chapter Eight

PRODEPENDENT RELATIONSHIPS

One of the basic rules of the universe is that nothing is perfect.
Perfection simply doesn't exist. Without imperfection,
neither you nor I would exist.

—Stephen Hawking

TWOS DON'T MARRY EIGHTS

I n 1979, writer/director Blake Edwards, known for great films like *Victor/Victoria* and *Breakfast at Tiffany's,* as well as the *Pink Panther* series, gave us a highly sexist but nonetheless wildly successful movie called *10*. This was the unlikely story of an average looking, somewhat idiotic middle-aged man (Dudley Moore) falling head over heels, at first sight, for his ideal woman (Bo Derek). As insulting to both sexes as this movie is today, it nevertheless introduced us to the idea of rating a person's physical attractiveness on a one to ten scale. In the film, Bo Derek is Dudley Moore's perfect ten. Very quickly, we all started to rate people in this way, and we still do it today. Over the years we've come to understand that twos don't tend to marry eights, except in cases where money, power, or some other form of status shifts the equation.

As we do with physical appearance, we can also give ourselves and others an emotional rating of one to ten. And once again we can state, rather unequivocally, that twos don't tend to partner with eights. That said, whether we are talking about physical appearance or emotional stability, our ratings are highly subjective. A person who rates a ten on my scale, either physically or emotionally, may be a three on someone else's scale, and someone who rates a ten on their scale may be a three on mine. It's all a matter of what we're looking for.

This is easier to understand with physical appearance. In the movie *10*, Dudley Moore thought Bo Derek was the most beautiful woman in the world. Meanwhile, my friend Nathan, a self-described "chubby chaser," described Bo Derek as "a disgusting bag of bones" while salivating over the Rubenesque woman who worked at his local donut shop. Dudley Moore and Nathan had very different versions of what a ten looks like. And that is not unusual. As my grandma used to say, "There's a lid for every pot."

In terms of emotional health, the same equation tends to hold true. Sam, for example, grew up in a highly dysfunctional home with a mother who was sometimes loving and intelligent, and sometimes running naked down the street screaming about the people trying to kill her. Because of this, Sam learned very early in life to continually monitor the moods of people around him and to modulate his expressions and behaviors to mitigate any "craziness" he might encounter on a particular day. And this makes perfect sense. As a child, he adapted to his unpredictable environment as a way of surviving profound family dysfunction.

When I first met Sam in therapy, he expressed frustration with his dating experiences. He put it this way: "Considering how I grew up, you'd think I would want a calm, stable partnership with none of the chaos of my childhood. But when I meet a woman like that, all I can think about is getting the hell out because I find her so unbelievably boring. It's like I can't get away fast enough. But then I meet a woman who's bipolar, off her meds, and three days sober from meth, and I'm ready for the wedding after one date." Thus, Sam, though he continually told himself (and others) that he wanted a life nothing like the life he grew up with, found himself attracted to women who provided exactly that.

Sam's frustration is not unusual for people who've grown up in dysfunctional environments. As much as Sam thinks he wants a calm and stable partner, he finds that those women have no emotional resonance for him. He is just not attuned to that type of person. When he meets an attractive woman who is open, warm, loving, and doesn't create drama on a regular basis, he struggles to relate to and connect with her, or he finds her boring, or he behaves in ways that create the drama he seems to need, which of course pushes the less drama-centric woman away.

BIRDS OF A FEATHER . . .

A highly useful way to understand what Sam is going through is to consider the process of filial imprinting in birds. Filial imprinting occurs when a bird imprints on a parent and follows and mimics the

actions of that parent. (Think about chicks following a hen, or goslings following a goose.) Filial imprinting in birds gives them a sense
of species identification. They do not automatically know what they
are when they hatch, so they visually imprint on their parents, and
then they identify with their species for life.

That is the ideal version of filial imprinting in birds. But some
birds will imprint on humans. Ornithologist Konrad Lorenz found
that incubator-hatched geese will imprint on the first moving stimulus
they see after hatching. For example, Lorenz had geese imprinted on
him—or, more specifically, his wading boots. (He is often described
as having a gaggle of geese following him around his lab—as both
goslings and adults because geese imprint for life.) Lorenz even got a
batch of geese to imprint on a colorful box placed on a model train,
which they followed as it circled its track.

Humans, of course, are far more emotionally sophisticated than
chicks and goslings, but the concept of filial imprinting nonetheless
holds water. Birds imprint on the physical manifestations of whatever they see immediately after birth. Humans attune similarly, but
to more than just the first thing we see. We also imprint on powerful
emotional experiences. As infants, toddlers, and children, we learn
what it means to be taken care of, to feel stimulated, to be engaged,
to be validated, to be comforted, to be ignored, and all the rest. And
we carry that imprint with us in our adult lives—seeking relationships that evoke this imprint even if we intellectually might prefer
something else.

So, as stated earlier, emotional twos don't tend to partner with
emotional eights. Instead, we find people we can relate to and feel
comfortable with, people whose dysfunction mirrors or meshes with
our own. We do this because these are the people with whom we can

emotionally and psychologically connect, and, ideally, with whom we can emotionally and psychologically grow. As long as we are "close enough" on the one to ten scale of emotional wellness, we are right for one another.

As you may recall, I have defined prodependence as occurring when relationships are mutually beneficial, with one person's strengths filling in the weak points of the other, and vice versa, with this mutual support occurring automatically and without question. This tends to occur most easily when emotional eights partner with nines, or when threes partner with twos, or fives partner with fives, etc. If people are too far apart on the scale, they're not a good match, and they will struggle to stay bonded.

IMPRINTING IN THE CODEPENDENCE CONTEXT

The codependency model recognizes the fact that we seek what we know, that we imprint emotionally and seek to bond with "our species" as we grow into adults. However, instead of celebrating the fact that two emotional equivalents have come together in a relationship they can each handle, codependence blames nonaddicted partners for being emotionally unhealthy and partnering with other emotionally unhealthy people—people who are either already addicted or susceptible to addiction.

What codependence fails to acknowledge is that people tend to come together because they can relate to and connect with one another on a level that is comfortable and familiar. And usually two people will naturally stay at the same

> What codependence fails to acknowledge is that people tend to come together because they can relate to and connect with one another on a level that is comfortable and familiar.

emotional and psychological level or move up or down the scale slightly over time, which enables them to continue relating to and staying connected with one another.

However, some people do grow or regress over time. For instance, a person may become actively addicted, emotionally regressing from a seven to a three in the process. This can make it very difficult for the addict's partner and other family members to stay connected. Similarly, one partner in a relationship might recognize problems and seek treatment, embarking on a process of serious emotional growth and progressing from an emotional three to a seven. When this occurs without the other partner also entering a process of healing and growth, the couple can "grow apart."

The good news is that if both parties in a relationship are willing to grow over time, both individually and together, issues can be overcome and a pair of emotional fives can turn into emotional eights. But they must each be willing to grow as individuals while simultaneously tolerating (and supporting) their partner's growth.

IMPRINTING IN THE PRODEPENDENCE CONTEXT

Prodependent relationships are a matter of finding the partner that fits us best, and, when necessary, growing over time *with that partner*. This is a far cry from the "detach with love" advice we tend to hear with codependence. Detach with love typically means that we work on ourselves and leave our addicted loved one to his or her own devices. When reframed using the prodependence model, however, we can happily and healthfully do what comes naturally to us as human beings. We can continue to love and support the addict, but in ways that are more helpful to the addict, while doing a better job of making sure our own needs are met. If the addict is willing to grow as we grow, there is hope.

Like it or not, the dynamics of love and connection that we experience and learn in childhood from our parents affect our later-life relationship choices, as well as how we behave within those relationships. This is neither good nor bad, right nor wrong. It just is.

Viewing life through the lens of prodependence, partners of addicts can say:

- Maybe it's not true that I'm partnered with the wrong person and that's why I'm unhappy.
- Maybe it's not true that I'm doomed to only spend time with losers.
- Maybe if I approach my addicted loved one differently, as I seek growth on my part, he or she will choose to grow with me.
- Maybe the attachment I feel to my addicted loved one is not crazy or unhealthy.
- Maybe I'm not messed up to the point where I can never hope for better than what I've got.

We are all wounded in one way or another. No one makes it to adult life without some well-earned emotional and psychological battle scars. Some of us have more of these scars than others, of course. And that's OK. It doesn't mean we're inherently broken or unlovable; it simply means we are

We are all wounded in one way or another. No one makes it to adult life without some well-earned emotional and psychological battle scars. Some of us have more of these scars than others, of course. And that's OK. It doesn't mean we're inherently broken or unlovable; it simply means we are more likely to bond with people who are similarly wounded because *these are our people.*

more likely to bond with people who are similarly wounded because *these are our people.* We get them, we understand them, we can relate to them, and they to us. We provide and can tolerate (and even thrive in) one another's challenges.

Who cares if we found each other at the scratch and dent sale? We found each other. And we connected. And now, even if it's only because addiction is forcing us to do so, we can grow and become emotionally healthier together. Because we fit. Our relationship is and can continue to be mutually beneficial, with one person's strengths filling in the weak points of the other, and vice versa. Even when our strengths and weaknesses evolve over time.

PRODEPENDENCE IS NOT ONE SIZE FITS ALL

Healthy human attachment does not look the same for every person. It differs, sometimes quite a lot, based on not just trauma, but genetics, social background, technological fluency, and gender, among other factors.

- **Genetics.** The impact of genetics on personality, especially on aspects of connection, attachment, and dependence, is not well understood. We do, however, know that certain heritable personality traits affect a person's behavior, including issues like impulsivity[1] and susceptibility to emotional and psychological issues such as depression,[2] anxiety,[3] and addiction.[4] At the very least, these well-established genetic traits can indirectly influence a person's comfort level with connection, attachment, and dependence, potentially altering that person's comfort zone on the spectrum of dependency.

- **Social Background.** The explicit and implicit lessons learned from parents, religion, racial and ethnic background, and general social milieu affect a person's ability to relate to and connect with others throughout life. For example, a person may have been raised in a perfectly loving and supportive home where affection was not openly displayed. If so, that individual may choose to display affection and attachment less openly and comfortably than a person raised in a more demonstrative environment.

- **Reliance on and Fluency with Technology.** As little as a few years ago, I would not have listed technology as impacting a person's comfort level with attachment. In our increasingly digital world, however, meaningful connection and the provision of support can look very different for different people. For example, for younger individuals, online connections can be (and often are) as emotionally impactful as real-world interactions, while older individuals typically don't experience that. Either way, the use of technology can affect the way in which a person experiences attachment. Some people will use tech to feel connected, appreciated, supported, and loved, while others will use it as a buffer that helps them interact without becoming vulnerable (and, therefore, without developing true intimacy).

- **Gender.** In a general way, women tend to be more empathetic and community-based than men, with men being more analytical and willing to go it alone than women. Because of these basic differences, men's comfort levels with intimate attachment tend to be slightly lower.

The point I am making here is that not everyone can or should try to become what might appear to a casual observer to be "emotionally healthy." Emotional health is highly subjective, depending on the individual. What looks like an emotional three to you might look like an emotional ten to me, and that's the way it is.

We are who we are. Sure, we can tinker at the edges and slowly make healthy progress, learning to behave in ways that better serve us and our loved ones, but we cannot change our essential selves. If we're skittish about attachment, so be it, as long as we're not completely alone and isolated in ways that leave us feeling bereft and unsupported. If we're naturally a caregiver, that's great, as long as we're not overdoing it and stifling or smothering the people we care for.

At the end of the day, healthy emotional connection—prodependence—looks different for every person and every relationship. Recognizing this, it is important for therapists, especially early in the healing process, to meet clients where they are, including their comfort level with attachment. From that starting point, we can help them work their way toward prodependence, whatever that might look like *for them*. Along the way, clients and their loved ones can continue to fill in each other's weak spots in ways that are healthy *for them*.

A SUMMARY OF PRODEPENDENCE

Like addicts, loved ones of addicts typically have (occasionally extensive) trauma histories. But for them trauma hasn't completely poisoned the well of attachment, which is why they keep trying to help and to connect with the addict. It's also why trying to apply a trauma-based model of healing to loved ones of addicts tends to get wonky.

For caregiving loved ones of addicts, attachment is desirable and important. No matter how badly they've been traumatized, they're still reaching out and trying to connect. They may be doing this in unhelpful ways because that's what their early life family dysfunction and trauma

> For caregiving loved ones of addicts, attachment is desirable and important. No matter how badly they've been traumatized, they're still reaching out and trying to connect.

taught them to do, but they're still trying. And telling them they're traumatized and damaged and making bad decisions and entering bad relationships and staying in bad relationships because they're messed up by trauma *does not help them or give them a sense of hope.* Instead, it feels blaming and shaming, and it tends to drive them away from the help they need.

Addicts need their bad behavior and its underlying causes brought into the light. Addicts need their denial about what they're doing, why they're doing it, and the problems this is causing to be shattered. Caregiving loved ones of addicts? Not so much. Instead of confrontation and giant doses of reality, they need validation, loving support, and guidance for moving forward in ways that don't enmesh, enable, or control.

Talking to loved ones early in the healing process about things like early life trauma and how that's affecting their present-day behaviors is not an effective tactic. We need a different approach with caregiving loved ones—a treatment model that recognizes and celebrates their desire and need for attachment as a strength they can use for healing.

That model is prodependence.

Once again, this does not mean that loved ones of addicts don't have their own struggles based in trauma. They do. But trauma is not what causes them to stay with the addict, or to caretake the addict.

So, instead of pointing out their trauma and how it pushes them into unhealthy behaviors, we need to put our arms around them and commiserate while giving them tools for self-care, better boundaries, and healthier relating. Yes, we do need to identify and acknowledge the trauma wrought by the addiction. But digging deeper into a caregiving loved one's history in the early stages of healing is counterproductive. Caregivers don't respond to this because they're not ready to hear about it or deal with it. That's just not where they are.

Yes, loved ones of addicts are part of the system that perpetuates the addiction, but telling them that too early in the healing process causes them to feel blamed and shamed, greatly increasing the likelihood that they will turn away from much-needed assistance. If we approach these individuals from an attachment perspective where we affirm them and validate them, however, they tend to respond positively. They stick around, they do the work, they make changes, and they heal. With the attachment-based prodependence model we, as therapists, can do a significant amount of desperately needed behaviorally focused crisis and intervention work without forcing loved ones into deeper issues before they are ready.

When treating loved ones of addicts, we can approach them from love or fear. Prodependence comes from love, love, and more love. Just as the caregiver comes from love. More important, prodependence meets the caregiver where he or she is, using language that he or she can understand and identify with. And it does this without blaming, judging, or pathologizing, instead offering empathy, concern, boundaries, comfort, and direction.

Prodependence FAQs

Codependence: a trauma-based theory of human dependency which, by definition, states that those who partner with an active addict do so as a form of trauma repetition—putting themselves in a relationship where the other person's needs will eventually exceed and overwhelm their own. These caretakers, by definition, demonstrate their trauma-based low self-esteem and desperate desire for approval by seeking out and becoming deeply attached to such troubled people, feeling that they can resolve the addict's problems.

Prodependence: an attachment-based theory of human dependency which, by definition, states that those who partner with an active addict are loving people caught up in circumstances beyond their ability to healthfully cope. Moreover, their desire to help the addict and all related actions toward helping the addict demonstrate nothing more than a normal and healthy attempt to remain connected to a failing loved one while facing extraordinarily difficult circumstances.

Q: Why change things? What was wrong with codependence?

A: I wrote this book because I have seen too many addicts' loved ones turn away from desperately needed direction and support because they couldn't or wouldn't accept the codependence tenet that being in this situation automatically implies there is something wrong *with them*. Meanwhile, their chronically addicted partner, parent, or child is failing at school, getting fired from another job, or getting arrested. I have seen many good therapists lacking useful answers to help such family members and caregivers. Often, the therapist's only choice is to rely on models such as codependence, which feels more negative and alienating than invitational. Now, with prodependence, they have another option. Prodependence recognizes the inherent grace of these caregivers, applauding and appreciating their unconditional love, their courage, and their conviction in trying to support some of the most challenged among us.

Q: What is the major difference between codependence and prodependence?

A: *Codependence* is a model of human behavior based in *trauma theory*. To "be codependent" implies that one tends to bond deeply with those with whom interactions often mirror early traumatic deficits. Failure on the part of the active addict then serves as a trigger for the nonaddicted partner to act out his or her unmet needs or abuse from childhood within this troubled adult relationship. Codependence implies that the loved ones of addicts, due to their underlying, often unconscious "childhood issues" tend to, as adults, give too much and love too much. Thus, they attract, enable, and enmesh with addicted partners. The goals of codependency treatment revolve around themes of detachment, self-actualization, becoming less needy, and working through past trauma to become more aware, less enabling, and less accepting of troubled, emotionally unavailable people. *Prodependence* is a model of human behavior based in *attachment theory*. To "be prodependent" implies that one is able to create deep, bonded adult attachments that mirror our very human, normative longings for healthy dependence and intimacy. Prodependence assumes that, when one loves and bonds deeply, it is natural and therefore non-pathological to do whatever it takes to ensure the safety and stability of those with whom one is attached. Prodependence implies that loved ones of addicts, regardless of prior history, will take extraordinary measures to keep those they love stable and to ensure the safety of their families. There is no pathology assigned to loving in prodependence. Rather, prodependence asserts that loving addicts or other chronically troubled people healthfully requires a different form of love than that with healthy adults. Loving prodependently requires support, guidance, and informed help.

Q: When did codependence evolve into theory and practice?

A: Codependence was initially promoted in six books published between 1981 and 1989, mostly written by female therapists who worked in the addiction field. It meshed with and ultimately subsumed the preexisting co-addiction movement. And later it broadened in the larger culture to include caregivers of all stripes, not just caregivers of addicts.

Q: Why did codependence become so popular?

A: Codependence was an easy-to-understand, engaging concept, and it mirrored the culture of the era of its creation. This is explained in detail in chapters 2 and 3 of this book.

Q: Can codependence treatment be counterproductive when working with loved ones of addicts?

A: Yes, and it frequently is. Codependence, by definition, implies that there is something wrong with the person who loves, rescues, helps, and cares for an addict. This is especially true if that person has given up essential parts of himself or herself in the process. Embracing the codependence model requires loved ones of addicts, who are already in crisis, to accept that there is something wrong *with them* that they need to fix. This can lead to caregivers feeling misunderstood and judged. As a result, many leave treatment before they receive the help they desperately need.

Q: Is this book suggesting that codependency doesn't exist?

A: Yes. Prodependence, as a concept and in practice, does not support the concept of codependence. Prodependence sees codependence as a theory that does not fully encompass the lived experience of addicts' loved ones, nor take into account the needs of the situations they face with an active addict. Execution of the codependence model in treatment tends to alienate the people it was designed to help, as it leaves them feeling more judged than supported. Additionally, the theory of codependence has never been formalized as a clinical diagnosis. In fact, it was proposed and rejected by the APA.

Q: **How does prodependence view the problem behaviors acted out by an addict's loved ones, such as enabling, overzealously caretaking, and even raging at the addict?**

A: Prodependence views all such activity as the caregiver's "best attempt" to save a troubled loved one. It sees these behaviors as loving—though often less than ideal—efforts to save a person they care for. These behaviors are viewed as problematic only due to their ineffectiveness and potential to escalate the problems they were intended to solve. However, prodependence does not label or judge the loved one who engages in such behaviors. Instead, prodependence views these actions as a loved one's best effort to stay connected and help in a situation that is far beyond his or her ability to remedy.

Q: **How does prodependence tackle typical challenges to treating loved ones of addicts, including emotional reactivity and enabling?**

A: Prodependence considers the fact that loved ones usually lack the specialized training or education that would equip them to work with an out-of-control, addicted person. It also recognizes the immense pain and fear that comes along with witnessing a beloved family member fail. These individuals often compensate for their lack of expertise with passionate attempts to help their loved one, but, because of the lack of proper training, their efforts are often not useful and can at times be counterproductive. In prodependence, the therapist does not pathologize family members' attempts to heal someone they love. They are not regarded as anything but loving, even when their attempts fail.

The goal is to support family members by validating their love while simultaneously developing skills that help to make their loving more effective and useful. These skills include, but are not limited to, setting boundaries, caring for oneself, and, when useful, detachment.

Q: **Does prodependence say that there is nothing wrong with the loved ones of an addict, even when they exhibit problematic traits?**

A: Prodependence implies that such loved ones of addicts are caught up in circumstances, such as witnessing the emotional decline of a beloved family member, that would naturally overwhelm anyone. Thus, there is nothing "wrong" with them, in terms of relating to the addict, regardless of their personal history. They are trying as best they can to survive and to help their family to survive extraordinary, overwhelming circumstances. What these caregivers require from early treatment is validation for the love and care they have given, in addition to supportive and clear directions about loving their troubled family member in healthier ways. That said, loved ones of addicts may in fact have underlying trauma and other issues that they might eventually want to address. (See the next three questions for more on this topic.)

Q: **What about trauma? Don't many spouses of addicts have early childhood trauma?**

A: Yes, many spouses of addicts, much like addicts themselves, have had early or later-life traumatic experiences. In fact, these similar histories, both conscious and unconscious, are frequently part of what has bonded these people to one another. And some partners may act out elements of past trauma in the acute stages of the addict's problems. This is unsurprising, considering the extremely stressful and overwhelming circumstances addictions produce. That said, many spouses of addicts and alcoholics lack any traumatic history of their own. Either way, initial therapy and treatment for partners of addicts, utilizing the prodependence model, does not seek to investigate such issues. Instead, the intention is to address the problems that these partners are currently attempting to solve.

Q: **How does prodependence view and treat past trauma in partners of addicts?**

A: Prodependence sees an addict's partner as being in crisis when beginning treatment. Therefore, all treatment is intended to help this individual resolve his or her immediate crisis. After the crisis has been addressed, the client is encouraged to examine his or her personal history with the therapist, should he or she display an interest. However, prodependence does not bind the reactions of someone living with an active addict to his or her past. Asking a partner to address trauma—or even to examine his or her own history—early in the recovery process can actually be abusive, as doing so implies an innate fault with the caregiver. Thus, this is not a priority early in the partner's treatment.

Q: **What happens when a partner of an alcoholic or addict appears so emotionally disabled that he or she is actively interfering with the process of healing the addiction?**

A: If the partner is unable to be soothed, supported, or redirected in early addiction treatment, this simply implies that he or she needs care that is separate and apart from his or her relationship with the addict. These are often familiar and diagnosable

conditions—exhibited as a result of living under profound stress—
such as depression, anxiety, or the triggering of traumatic events in
the partner's past. As these individuals heal, their treatment can then
be integrated into overall addiction family care.

Q: **What about the apparent need of "codependent" people,
in general, to self-actualize and grow, independent of their
relationships and bonds?**

A: Prodependence, coming from an attachment-based perspective, says that all of us are deeply dependent on one another
for emotional survival and, further, that this is a good thing. Mutual,
deep, and enduring dependencies from womb to tomb is how humans
survive and thrive; as such, relationships should never be regarded as
inherently pathological. Prodependence celebrates rather than pathologizes deep emotional dependency. It regards healthy, deeply bonded
relationships of all kinds as key to an individual's self-actualization.
Enmeshment is viewed merely as an inadequate attempt at loving. An
individual practicing enmeshment requires new skills to improve his
or her relationships.

Q: **What about those who are so needy and desperate in close
relationships that they become unable to function without
one? Aren't they deeply codependent?**

A: For several decades, the Diagnostic and Statistical Manual of
Mental Disorders (the DSM) has had a fully fleshed out, cri-
teria-based diagnosis for people who are so emotionally limited and
impaired that they "cling" to other people for their own emotional
stability. It's called Dependent Personality Disorder. Sadly, DPD and
codependence are often conflated.

Q: What kind of treatment should be offered to loved ones of addicts? Don't they still need help with boundaries, self-care, and managing their situations?

A: Any loving person in a meaningful relationship with an active addict is, by definition, in need of support. He or she likely needs encouragement toward both greater self-care and establishing healthy boundaries with their troubled loved one. However, no loving person in a meaningful relationship with an active addict should be asked to doubt the nature of his or her love or to question his or her own emotional stability in order to be taught such skills and to be given the support that he or she deserves.

Q: What do you say to the millions of people who have embraced the concept of codependence? Where does prodependence leave these individuals?

A: Taking the path of self-exploration and personal growth is a positive thing that strengthens individuals and society. I am certain that many of those who have embraced codependence have become better people for having done so; that is to be applauded. I would simply ask such individuals to reconsider the concept of "loving too much," as I think the phrase is demeaning. For example, you may love in the wrong ways for the wrong reasons. You may love in ways that don't achieve the result you seek. You may love and lose. You may love and hurt. However, you can never feel too much love, express too much compassion, or exhibit too much empathy. Claiming this is possible is counterintuitive to the realities of healthy human attachment and bonding. I also think it worth noting that a deepened intimacy with our partners and family members allows us to achieve a higher form self-actualization than is otherwise possible.

Endnotes

Preface

1 Darwin, C. (1909). *The origin of species*. Dent.

Chapter 1

1 Siegel, D. J. (2015). *The developing mind: How relationships and the brain interact to shape who we are*. Guilford Publications.

2 Black, C. (2002). *It will never happen to me: Growing up with addiction as youngsters, adolescents, adults*. Hazelden Publishing; Beattie, M. (1992). *Codependent no more: How to stop controlling others and start caring for yourself*. Hazelden Publishing; Mellody, P., Miller, A. W., & Miller, K. (1989). *Facing codependence: What it is, where it comes from, how it sabotages our lives*. Harper, San Francisco; Bradshaw, J. (2007). The Therapeutic Genius of Pia Mellody. *Cutting Edge*. Retrieved 6.11.18 from https://www.themeadows.com/blog/item/373-the-therapeutic-genius-of-pia-mellody; Norwood, R. (1986). *Women who love too much: When you keep wishing and hoping he'll change*. Simon and Schuster; Woititz, J. G. (1990). *Adult children of alcoholics: expanded edition*. Health Communications, Inc.; Woititz, J. G. (1986). *Marriage on the rocks: Learning to live with yourself and an alcoholic*. Health Communications; among other sources.

Chapter 2

1 Fischer, C. T. (1998). Phenomenological, existential, and humanistic foundations for psychology as a human science. *Comprehensive Clinical Psychology, 1*, 449–472.

2 Fischer, C. T. (1998). Phenomenological, existential, and humanistic foundations for psychology as a human science. *Comprehensive Clinical Psychology, 1*, 449–472.

3 Greening, T. (2006). Five basic postulates of humanistic psychology. *Journal of Humanistic Psychology, 46*(3), 239–239.

4   Courtois, C. A. (2014). *It's not you, it's what happened to you: Complex trauma and treatment.* Telemachus Press.

5   Courtois, C. A. (2014). *It's not you, it's what happened to you: Complex trauma and treatment.* Telemachus Press.

6   Anda, R., Felitti, V., Bremner, J., Walker, J., Whitfield, C., Perry, B., . . . Giles, W. (2006). The enduring effects of abuse and related adverse experiences in childhood. *European Archives of Psychiatry and Clinical Neuroscience, 256*(3), 174–186.

7   Bradshaw, J. (2005). *Healing the shame that binds you: Recovery classics edition.* Health Communications, Inc.

8   Friedan, B. (1963). *The feminine mystique.* W. W. Norton: New York.

9   Beattie, M. (1992). *Codependent no more: How to stop controlling others and start caring for yourself.* Hazelden Publishing.

10 Anderson, D. (1942). Alcohol and public opinion. *Quarterly Journal of Studies on Alcohol 3*(3), 376–392.

11 Mann, M. (1944). Formation of a National Committee for Education on Alcoholism. *Quarterly Journal of Studies on Alcohol, 5*(2), 354.

12 White, W. (2000). The rebirth of the disease concept of alcoholism in the 20th century. *Counselor, 1*(2), 62–66.

13 Saah, T. (2005). The evolutionary origins and significance of drug addiction. *Harm reduction journal, 2*(1), 8.

14 Maté, G. (2010). *In the realm of hungry ghosts: Close encounters with addiction.* North Atlantic Books.

15 Maté, G. (2010). *In the realm of hungry ghosts: Close encounters with addiction.* North Atlantic Books.

16 Jackson, J. (1962). Alcoholism and the family. In D. Pittman & C. Snyder (Eds.), *Society, Culture and Drinking Patterns,* pp. 472–492. New York: John Wiley & Sons; and, Chaudron, C. D. & Wilkinson, D. A., Eds. (1988). *Theories on alcoholism.* Addiction Research Foundation, pp. 297–298.

17 White, W., & Savage, B. (2005). All in the family: Alcohol and other drug problems, recovery, advocacy. *Alcoholism Treatment Quarterly, 23*(4), 3–37, citing Day, B. (1961). Alcoholism and the family. *Marriage and Family Living, 23,* 253–258, and, Reddy, B. (1971). *The family disease—alcoholism.* Unpublished Manuscript.

Chapter 3

1   Webster, M. (2006). Merriam-Webster online dictionary.

2   Cottrell, L. S., & Gallagher, R. (1941). Important developments in American social psychology during the past decade. *Sociometry, 4*(2), 107–139.

3 Alcoholics Anonymous, "AA Timeline," http://www.aa.org/pages/en_US/aa-timeline.

4 White, W. (2015). The vulnerability and resilience of children affected by addiction: Career reflections of Dr. Claudia Black, www.williamwhitepapers.com; and, Adult Children of Alcoholics (undated). Adult Children of Alcoholics and its Beginnings, http://www.adultchildren.org/lit-EarlyHistory.

5 Black, C. (1981). It Will Never Happen to Me: Children of Alcoholics as Youngsters —adolescents—adults. Ballantine Books.

6 Woititz, J. G. (1990). *Adult children of alcoholics: expanded edition.* Health Communications, Inc.

7 Norwood, R. (1986). *Women who love too much: When you keep wishing and hoping he'll change.* Simon and Schuster.

8 Cermak, T. L. (1986). *Diagnosing and treating co-dependence: A guide for professionals who work with chemical dependents, their spouses and children.* Johnson Institute Books.

9 Beattie, M. (1986). *Codependent no more: How to stop controlling others and start caring for yourself.* Hazelden.

10 Mellody, P., Miller, A. W., & Miller, J. K. (1989). Facing codependence: What it is, where it comes from, how it sabotages our lives. HarperCollins.

11 Beattie, M. (1986). *Codependent no more: How to stop controlling others and start caring for yourself.* Hazelden.

12 Cermak, T. L. (1986). Diagnostic criteria for codependency. *Journal of psychoactive drugs, 18*(1), 15–20.

13 Irvine, L. (1999). *Codependent forevermore: The invention of self in a twelve-step group.* University of Chicago Press.

14 Mellody, P., Miller, A. W., & Miller, J. K. (2003). *Facing codependence: What it is, where it comes from, how it sabotages our lives,* pp. xv and xvi. Harper Collins.

15 Beattie, M. (1992). *Codependent no more: How to stop controlling others and start caring for yourself.* Hazelden Publishing.

16 American Psychiatric Association. (2013). *Diagnostic and statistical manual of mental disorders (DSM-5®).* American Psychiatric Pub.

17 American Psychiatric Association. (2013). *Diagnostic and statistical manual of mental disorders (DSM-5®).* American Psychiatric Pub.

18 Wikipedia. Dependent Personality Disorder. Retrieved Mar 8, 2018 from https://en.wikipedia.org/wiki/Dependent_personality_disorder.

19 Beattie, M. (1992). *Codependent no more: How to stop controlling others and start caring for yourself.* Hazelden Publishing.

20 Rosenberg, R.A. (2018). *The human magnet syndrome: The codependent narcissist trap*. CreateSpace Independent Publishing.

21 Rosenberg, R. (2013). *The History of the Term Codependency*. https://blogs.psych central.com/human-magnets/2013/11/the-history-of-the-term-codependency/.

22 Beattie, M. (1992). *Codependent no more: How to stop controlling others and start caring for yourself*. Hazelden Publishing.

23 Beattie, M. (1992). *Codependent no more: How to stop controlling others and start caring for yourself*. Hazelden Publishing.

Chapter 4

1 Johnson, S. (2013). *Love sense: The revolutionary new science of romantic relationships*. Little, Brown.

2 Hawkley, L. C., Masi, C. M., Berry, J. D., & Cacioppo, J. T. (2006). Loneliness is a unique predictor of age-related differences in systolic blood pressure. *Psychology and Aging, 21*(1), 152; House, J. S., Landis, K. R., & Umberson, D. (1988). Social relationships and health. *Science, 241*(4865), 540; Kiecolt-Glaser, J. K., Malarkey, W. B., Chee, M., Newton, T., Cacioppo, J. T., Mao, H. Y., & Glaser, R. (1993). Negative behavior during marital conflict is associated with immunological down-regulation; *Psychosomatic Medicine, 55*(5), 395–409; Caspi, A., Harrington, H., Moffitt, T. E., Milne, B. J., & Poulton, R. (2006). Socially isolated children 20 years later: Risk of cardiovascular disease. *Archives of Pediatrics & Adolescent Medicine, 160*(8), 805–811; Thurston, R. C., & Kubzansky, L. D. (2009). Women, loneliness, and incident coronary heart disease. *Psychosomatic Medicine, 71*(8), 836; Hawkley, L. C., Masi, C. M., Berry, J. D., & Cacioppo, J. T. (2006). Lone-liness is a unique predictor of age-related differences in systolic blood pressure. *Psychology and Aging, 21*(1), 152; Hawkley, L. C., Thisted, R. A., Masi, C. M., & Cacioppo, J. T. (2010). Loneliness predicts increased blood pressure: 5-year cross-lagged analyses in middle-aged and older adults. *Psychology and Aging, 25*(1), 132; among other studies.

3 Vaillant, G. E. (2008). *Aging well: Surprising guideposts to a happier life from the landmark study of adult development*. Little, Brown; Johnson, S. (2008). *Hold me tight: Seven conversations for a lifetime of love*, p. 26. Little, Brown.

4 Coyne, J. C., Rohrbaugh, M. J., Shoham, V., Sonnega, J. S., Nicklas, J. M., & Cranford, J. A. (2001). Prognostic importance of marital quality for survival of congestive heart failure. *The American Journal of Cardiology, 88*(5), 526–529; Luo, Y., Hawkley, L. C., Waite, L. J., & Cacioppo, J. T. (2012). Loneliness, health, and mortality in old age: A national longitudinal study. *Social Science & Medicine, 74*(6), 907–914; Holt-Lunstad, J., Smith, T. B., & Layton, J. B. (2010). Social relationships and mortality risk: a meta- analytic review. *PLoS Medicine, 7*(7), e1000316; Patterson, A. C., & Veenstra, G. (2010). Loneliness and risk of mortality: A longitudinal investigation

in Alameda County, California. *Social Science & Medicine, 71*(1), 181–186; Peris-sinotto, C. M., Cenzer, I. S., & Covinsky, K. E. (2012). Loneliness in older persons: a predictor of functional decline and death. *Archives of Internal Medicine, 172*(14), 1078–1084; among other studies.

5   Bowlby, J. (1991). *Attachment and Loss* (Vol. 1). London: Penguin Books.

6   Spock, B. (1946). *The common-sense book of baby and child care.* New York: Duell, Sloan and Pearce.

7   Ainsworth, M. D. S., Blehar, M. C., Waters, E., & Wall, S. N. (2015). *Patterns of attachment: A psychological study of the strange situation.* Psychology Press.

8   Harlow, H. F. (1958). The nature of love. *American Psychologist, 13*(12), 673.

9   Tatkin, S. (2012). Wired for love: how understanding your partner's brain and attachment style can help you defuse conflict and build a secure relationship. New Harbinger Publications.

10   Coan, J. A., Schaefer, H. S., & Davidson, R. J. (2006). Lending a hand social regula-tion of the neural response to threat. *Psychological Science, 17*(12), 1032–1039.

11   Hawkley, L. C., Masi, C. M., Berry, J. D., & Cacioppo, J. T. (2006). Loneliness is a unique predictor of age-related differences in systolic blood pressure. *Psychology and Aging, 21*(1), 152.

12   Coyne, J. C., Rohrbaugh, M. J., Shoham, V., Sonnega, J. S., Nicklas, J. M., & Cranford, J. A. (2001). Prognostic importance of marital quality for survival of congestive heart failure. *The American Journal of Cardiology, 88*(5), 526–529.

13   Kiecolt-Glaser, J. K., Newton, T., Cacioppo, J. T., MacCallum, R. C., Glaser, R., & Malarkey, W. B. (1996). Marital conflict and endocrine function: Are men really more physiologically affected than women? *Journal of Consulting and Clinical Psy-chology, 64*(2), 324.

14   Cohen, S. (2001). Social relationships and susceptibility to the common cold. *Emo-tion, Social Relationships, and Health,* 221–223, and, Cohen, S., Doyle, W. J., Skoner, D. P., Rabin, B. S., & Gwaltney, J. M. (1997). Social ties and susceptibility to the common cold. *Jama, 277*(24), 1940–1944, x.

15   Pekovic, V., Seff, L., & Rothman, M. (2007). Planning for and responding to special needs of elders in natural disasters. *Generations, 31*(4), 37–41; and, Semenza, J. C., Rubin, C. H., Falter, K. H., Selanikio, J. D., Flanders, W. D., Howe, H. L., & Wilhelm, J. L. (1996). Heat-related deaths during the July 1995 heat wave in Chicago. *New England Journal of Medicine, 335*(2), 84–90.

16   House, J. S. (2001). Social isolation kills, but how and why? *Psychosomatic Medicine, 63*(2), 273–274.

17   Feeney, B. C. (2007). The dependency paradox in close relationships: Accepting dependence promotes independence. *Journal of Personality and Social Psychology, 92*(2), 268.

17 Johnson, S. (2008). *Hold me tight: Seven conversations for a lifetime of love*. Little, Brown.

Chapter 5

1 National Alliance on Mental Illness. Information retrieved from https://www.nami .org, May 29, 2018.

Chapter 6

1 Cheever, S. (2015). *Note found in a bottle*. Simon and Schuster.

2 Gura, P. F. (2007). *American transcendentalism: A history*. Macmillan.

3 Bejerot, N. (1980). Addiction to pleasure: A biological and social-psychological theory of addiction. *NIDA Research Monograph*, 30, 246.

4 US Department of Health and Human Services. (2009). Results from the 2007 National Survey on Drug Use and Health: Detailed Tables. *Substance Abuse and Mental Health Services Administration. SAMSHA, Office of AppliedStudies*.

5 Alexander, B. K., Beyerstein, B. L., Hadaway, P. F., & Coambs, R. B. (1981). Effect of early and later colony housing on oral ingestion of morphine in rats. *Pharmacology Biochemistry and Behavior*, 15(4), 571–576.

6 Hughes, C. E., & Stevens, A. (2010). What can we learn from the Portuguese decriminalization of illicit drugs? *British Journal of Criminology*, Information retrieved from https://doi.org/10.1093/bjc/azq038

Chapter 7

1 McGreevy, B. (2013). *Hemlock Grove*. FSG Originals.

2 Mays, M. *No Man's Land, Part I*. Retrieved Oct 5, 2017 from https://partnerhope .com/2017/06/no-mans-land-part-i/; and Mays, M. *No Man's Land, Part II*. Retrieved Oct 5, 2017 from https://partnerhope.com/2017/07/weathering-no-mans-land -part-2/.

Chapter 8

1 Anokhin, A. P., Grant, J. D., Mulligan, R. C., & Heath, A. C. (2015). The genetics of impulsivity: evidence for the heritability of delay discounting. Biological psychiatry, 77(10), 887–894.

2 Levinson, D. F. (2006). The genetics of depression: a review. Biological psychiatry, 60(2), 84–92.

3 Maier, W. (2003). Genetics of anxiety. Medical psychiatry, 21, 189–206.

4 Gelernter, J., & Kranzler, H. R. (2008). Genetics of addiction. The American psychiatric publishing textbook of substance abuse treatment, 17–27; Alsakaf, I., & Bhatia, S. C. (2017). Genetics of Addiction. Substance and Nonsubstance Related Addiction Disorder: Diagnosis and Treatment, 21; among other sources.

Index

Note: *b* indicates a box, *t* a table.

About the Author

Robert Weiss, PhD, MSW, CEO of Seeking Integrity LLC, is a digital-age sex, intimacy, and relationship specialist. Dr. Weiss has spent more than twenty-five years developing treatment programs, educating clinicians, writing, and providing direct care to those challenged by digital-age infidelity, sexual compulsivity, and other addictive disorders. A clinical sexologist, psychotherapist, and international educator, he frequently serves as a subject matter expert for multiple media outlets including CNN, HLN, MSNBC, Fox, OWN, *The New York Times, The Los Angeles Times,* and NPR, among others.

In addition to *Prodependence,* Dr. Weiss is the author of several highly regarded books on sex and intimacy disorders including *Out of the Doghouse, Sex Addiction 101,* and *Cruise Control,* among others. His *Psychology Today* blog, "Love and Sex in the Digital Age," has over 8 million readers to date. He also podcasts (Sex, Love, & Addiction 101) and hosts a free, weekly interactive sex and intimacy webinar via *SexandRelationshipHealing.com.*

A skilled clinical educator, Dr. Weiss has created and overseen more than a dozen high-end addiction and mental health treatment programs in the US and abroad. As CEO of Seeking Integrity LLC, he is actively working to create easily accessed, useful, online and real-world solutions that anyone struggling with sex, intimacy, and relationship concerns can utilize. His current project, *SexandRelationshipHealing.com*, is an extensive online resource for recovery from sex and intimacy disorders.

For more information or to reach Dr. Weiss, please visit his website, *RobertWeissMSW.com*, or follow him on Twitter (@RobWeissMSW), LinkedIn (Robert Weiss LCSW), and Facebook (Rob Weiss MSW).